Elizabeth Rusch

Photos by **Karin Anderson**

IMPACT!

ASTEROIDS AND THE SCIENCE
OF SAVING THE WORLD

HOUGHTON MIFFLIN HARCOURT

Boston New York

OF THE UNIVERSE WITH ME. —E.R.

The text of this book is set in Weiss.

Library of Congress Cataloging-in-Publication Data
Names: Rusch, Elizabeth, author. | Anderson, Karin, illustrator.
Title: Impact!: asteroids and the science of saving the world /
by Elizabeth Rusch; photos by Karin Anderson.
Other titles: Scientists in the field.
Description: Boston ; New York : Houghton Mifflin Harcourt, 2017. |
Series: Scientists in the field series | Audience: Ages 10–12. |
Audience: Grades 4 to 6.
Identifiers: LCCN 2016030626 | ISBN 9780544671591 (hardcover)
Subjects: LCSH: Asteroids—Collisions with Earth
—Juvenile literature. | Asteroids—Juvenile literature. |
Meteorites—Juvenile literature. |
Extinction (Biology)—Juvenile literature.
Classification: LCC QB651 .R87 2017 | DDC 551.3/97—dc23

CONTENTS

M. Ahmetvaleev, a local resident, shot this photograph of an asteroid streaking across the sky above Chelyabinsk, Russia, on February 15, 2013.

Chapter One

AN ASTEROID STRIKES

On February 15, 2013, the sun rose into a soft blue sky over the Russian city of Chelyabinsk. People bundled up tightly against the freezing weather and crunched their way through the snow past the low concrete buildings and warehouses. At 9:20 a.m., some of them noticed a strange bright point, high in the sky. It slowly grew bigger and bigger. Two smoky trails followed behind.

The fourth grade students of School No. 37 were settling in for the day with a substitute teacher, Yulia Karbysheva. Suddenly an intense flash, like a second sun, blazed across the sky.

The fourth-graders rushed to the window to see what it was.

Yulia had no idea what was happening. She yelled to her students: *Duck and cover!* The children crawled under their desks and wrapped their arms around their heads.

The Chelyabinsk fireball flashed with a blinding light as it blasted through the atmosphere at more than 40,000 miles (70,000 km) per hour.

Then—*ka-bang! crash!*—glass exploded in through the classroom windows, slicing Yulia's leg and arm. Her forty-four students cowered under their desks, unharmed. More explosions —*bam, bam, bam,* like gunshots—blasted across the whole city. Chaos erupted.

Buildings rattled, roofs collapsed, and windows shattered, spraying glass shards everywhere. Doors banged open, furniture shook, and dishes flew across rooms and smashed to pieces.

People screamed and panicked. Car alarms blared, adding to the confusion.

Reports from all over Chelyabinsk flooded social media.

"We got an awful jolt, like an earthquake," one person wrote.

"Windows were blown out, furniture was jumping. I am shaking now," another reported.

"It is a nightmare," a third witness shared. "I am still young; I don't want to die!"

Some people thought a nuclear bomb had exploded or a

The shock wave from the Chelyabinsk asteroid shattered windows all across the city. Employees survey the damage done to the foyer of the Chelyabinsk Drama Theatre.

war had begun. "My heart is still beating two hundred heartbeats a minute," one mother wrote on a local web forum. "I saw this terrible flash, it was red-orange! My eyes are still hurting. I turned off all the lights, sat my kids on the couch and waited. Oh my God, I thought the war has begun."

A clue about what really happened lay more than fifty miles (80 km) away in the middle of a frozen lake in the Siberian wilderness. People nearby had followed the ball of light as it soared across the sky. They trudged across the snow-covered ice until they came to an eerie sight: a twenty-foot-wide (6 m) round hole in the thick ice. As they peered into the dark water, someone joked: "Now green men will crawl out and say hello."

No aliens sprang from the hole, but the locals were right—the flash and blasts were caused by an object from outer space. An asteroid the size of a six-story building and heavier than the Eiffel Tower had careened toward Earth and exploded in the sky. The largest piece left, about the size of a chair, had landed on the bottom of the lake. Thousands of smaller pieces littered the ground for miles.

No one saw the Chelyabinsk asteroid coming, yet scientists have a good idea of how it got there. Most asteroids that approach Earth come from the main asteroid belt, an area where millions of the huge space rocks orbit the sun between Mars and Jupiter.

A chair-size chunk of the Chelyabinsk asteroid busted a hole through the thick ice of Lake Chebarkul.

These two fragments of the Chelyabinsk meteorite were found in a field between two villages outside the city. The broken fragment shows a light-colored interior and the dark fusion crust formed during the rock's fiery journey though the atmosphere. The unbroken fragment on the right shows a complete fusion crust.

Asteroids in the belt between Mars and Jupiter generally stay there for *billions* of years. But sometimes an asteroid is bumped out of the belt by the gravitational pull of objects around it, from a collision, or even from the pressure of sunlight on its surface. When this happens, the asteroid's orbit becomes unstable and it can begin to swing near Earth. Within a few million years, most near-Earth asteroids will do one of three things: crash into the sun; get pushed out of the solar system; or crash into a planet, perhaps Earth.

Scientists think the Chelyabinsk asteroid originated during the birth of the solar system some 4.6 billion years ago in the main belt. About a million years ago, a chunk of rock broke off or spun off from a larger asteroid. Orbiting objects move very fast, so the huge rock hurtled toward our planet at

THANK YOU, ATMOSPHERE!

The Earth is getting pummeled by small fragments of asteroids all the time, and most of the time no one notices. That's because the atmosphere does a really good job protecting us.

How does something so light and airy protect us? The atmosphere is a layer of gases around the planet, held in place by gravity. When an asteroid comes screaming through the atmosphere, the gases compress around it quickly, heating and incinerating the object. The atmosphere is like a giant laser, blasting apart anything that flies fast into it.

While some larger objects can get through, they rarely cause much damage. Why? Because the Earth's surface is mostly covered by vast oceans, asteroids that manage to make it through the atmosphere will most likely hit water.

forty thousand miles (64,374 km) per hour, about fifty times the speed of sound.

When the asteroid slammed into our atmosphere in 2013, friction slowed and heated the rock until its outer surface began to melt and vaporize. At about twenty-five miles (40 km) above the Earth, large chunks began cracking off. The pressure grew and grew as the asteroid hurtled toward the ground until it exploded in a blinding flash, pushing a shock wave more powerful than thirty atomic bombs toward the city. Though the Chelyabinsk asteroid was relatively small and the atmos-phere prevented it from hitting the Earth intact, the extent of the damage was frightening.

The blast injured more than 1,500 people, mostly by knocking them to the ground or cutting them with flying debris, as happened to fourth grade teacher Yulia Karbysheva. Pressure from the shock wave damaged more than seven thousand buildings—including 360 schools. Destruction stretched sixty miles (100 km) out from the city.

Luckily, the asteroid wasn't bigger—or made of something really hard and strong, like iron. Luckily, the asteroid broke apart in the atmosphere before the massive rock could smash into the city. Luckily, no one died.

We may not be so lucky the next time.

Many more asteroids approach Earth than you might imagine. Every minute of every day the Earth is pummeled by rocks and particles from space —*one hundred tons of space rocks* daily. That's the equivalent of a hundred pickup truck loads. Usu-

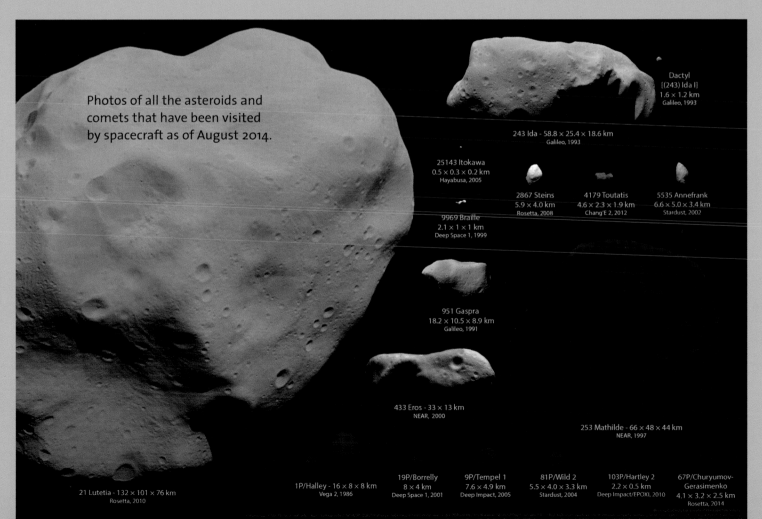

Photos of all the asteroids and comets that have been visited by spacecraft as of August 2014.

Dactyl
[(243) Ida I]
1.6 × 1.2 km
Galileo, 1993

243 Ida - 58.8 × 25.4 × 18.6 km
Galileo, 1993

25143 Itokawa
0.5 × 0.3 × 0.2 km
Hayabusa, 2005

2867 Steins
5.9 × 4.0 km
Rosetta, 2008

4179 Toutatis
4.6 × 2.3 × 1.9 km
Chang'E 2, 2012

5535 Annefrank
6.6 × 5.0 × 3.4 km
Stardust, 2002

9969 Braille
2.1 × 1 × 1 km
Deep Space 1, 1999

951 Gaspra
18.2 × 10.5 × 8.9 km
Galileo, 1991

433 Eros - 33 × 13 km
NEAR, 2000

253 Mathilde - 66 × 48 × 44 km
NEAR, 1997

21 Lutetia - 132 × 101 × 76 km
Rosetta, 2010

1P/Halley - 16 × 8 × 8 km
Vega 2, 1986

19P/Borrelly
8 × 4 km
Deep Space 1, 2001

9P/Tempel 1
7.6 × 4.9 km
Deep Impact, 2005

81P/Wild 2
5.5 × 4.0 × 3.3 km
Stardust, 2004

103P/Hartley 2
2.2 × 0.5 km
Deep Impact/EPOXI, 2010

67P/Churyumov-
Gerasimenko
4.1 × 3.2 × 2.5 km
Rosetta, 2014

An artist's concept of collisions that took place during the birth of our solar system.

THE BIRTH OF THE SOLAR SYSTEM—AND THE ASTEROID BELT

Roughly 4.6 billion years ago, when the solar system was beginning to develop, gases, dust, and bits of rock and metal began to pull toward each other from the force of their gravity. Small bits clung together, creating bigger chunks. Over time some grew ever larger and rounder, eventually collecting everything in their path and becoming our planets.

The rocky planets clustered close to the sun while the gaseous planets dominated the outer solar system. When Jupiter took shape, its gravity prevented some of the huge rocks in the gap between itself and Mars from growing any larger. Instead, the bodies smashed into each other, breaking into fragments. Today these irregularly shaped blobs of rock, metal, and dust—called asteroids—circle the sun, spinning in the belt as they orbit.

Many modern television and movie scenes give us the impression that the asteroid belt and other asteroid fields in the universe are thickly littered with rocks. In the movie *The Empire Strikes Back*, Han Solo flies through an asteroid field jam-packed so tightly with rocks that spacecraft pursuing him get smashed between them. On *Star Trek*, the ensign of the starship *Enterprise* also has to dodge and weave to make it through asteroid belts.

But the truth is, most of the asteroid belt is just cold, black, empty space. If you put all the rocks in the belt together, they would make a tiny mass, much smaller than our moon. And this material is spread out over an enormous area, like a few rubber ducks floating in a huge ocean. In fact, if you were standing on one asteroid, other asteroids would just look like faint stars, if you could see them at all.

ally the "rocks" are space dust no bigger than grains of sand that are obliterated in a bright flash of light, when they hit the atmosphere. We call these streaks of light falling stars; scientists call them meteors.

But many asteroids careening through our solar system are much bigger and have the potential to cause much more damage. Astronomers estimate that the asteroid belt alone holds more than two hundred asteroids at least sixty miles (100 km) wide. More than 750,000 are a half mile (800 m) across or wider. Smaller asteroids, like the one that struck Chelyabinsk, number in the *millions*.

About once a year, a car-size asteroid strikes the Earth. Most of these blow up in the atmosphere like Chelyabinsk without causing much damage. But roughly every five thousand years, the Earth is struck by an asteroid as big as a football field. And every few million years, an asteroid large enough to trigger global disasters strikes.

That's why a group of dedicated scientists are working as fast as they can to understand the dangers these space rocks pose, to track any that might be on a collision course with Earth, and to create a way to stop them before it's too late. The quest begins with the search for pieces of asteroids that land on the ground, called meteorites, which can tell us more about these strange and potentially dangerous space rocks.

ASTEROID: A rock, smaller than a planet, orbiting the sun (also known as a planetoid or minor planet).

NEAR-EARTH ASTEROID (NEA): An asteroid with an orbit that brings it between the sun and 1.3 times the distance between the sun and Earth (or 1.3 astronomical units).

POTENTIALLY HAZARDOUS ASTEROID (PHA): An asteroid larger than 500 feet (150 meters) across, with an orbit that will bring it within about 45 million miles of Earth's orbit. It's big enough to cause widespread destruction—and close enough that a change in orbit could nudge it into a collision course with Earth.

SUN

Earth, NEA, and PHA orbits (not to scale)

EARTH'S ATMOSPHERE

FIREBALL: A meteor that shines more brightly than Venus.

METEOR SHOWER: When multiple meteors appear in the same part of the sky in the same night.

METEOR: The flash of light when an asteroid hits our atmosphere and burns up from friction.

METEORITE: A piece of an asteroid that survives passage through the atmosphere and lands on the surface of the earth.

EARTH

Chapter Two
CLUES ON THE GROUND

Roughly 350 times each year, asteroids careen through the atmosphere and scatter meteorites on the Earth's surface. "If you happened to be standing where a meteorite fall occurred, you probably wouldn't see rocks falling from the sky, but you'd hear them," says Marc Fries, a research scientist with NASA's Johnson Space Center in Houston, Texas, and a curator of space rocks for NASA. "There would be a big *boom* and a bunch of smaller booms from rocks moving at supersonic speeds. About two minutes later—*whomp!*—a big one would hit the ground hard. Maybe a few more. Then smaller rocks would fall all around, sounding like machine-gun fire: *TAT, TAT, tat, tat, tat, tat, tat*. Rocks would continue to drop

More than two hundred people reported a fireball over these hills near Creston, California. One witness saw something flash blue as it entered the atmosphere with a long orange, yellow, and red trail that came to a point. "It was like a huge firework as it broke apart," she reported. "We heard what sounded like bombs dropping and then a long rumble followed. [The] sound went on for over a minute."

for up to about ten minutes, getting smaller and smaller: *POP, POP, pop, pop, pop, pop, pop."*

Each of these rocks is a precious packet of information that can help scientists better understand asteroids and the danger they pose—if the researchers can get their hands on them.

Finding newly fallen meteorites, and finding them quickly, is a challenge. "Meteorite falls are not terribly rare, but actually recovering the meteorites from fresh falls is very rare," says Marc. In fact, the vast majority of meteorites that hit our planet are never found. About half fall during daylight and go unnoticed. Seventy percent fall into the ocean where they can't be recovered. And it doesn't take much in the way of terrain or plant cover to hide the others.

But those odds don't deter professional meteorite hunters like Robert Ward, who will hop on a plane from his home in

HOW ARE FALLING ROCKS LIKE RAIN?

Marc Fries, a NASA scientist, has developed an ingenious method to narrow the possible landing area of meteorites, called the strewn field. Rocks falling through the sky look similar to rainfall in Doppler weather radar images. When witnesses report a fireball, Marc collects weather radar images from that time and location to track the rocks as they plummet through the sky. Using estimates of the speed and direction of the rocks as they dropped, he creates a map of where meteorites may have landed.

In this map of the strewn field he made of a Creston, California, fireball, red indicates the estimated fall area of meteorites that are 2.2 pounds (1 kg) or larger. Orange shows estimated landing areas for meteorites less than a pound (in the hundreds of grams), and yellow shows meteorites smaller than two teaspoons (1–10 g). The entire strewn field is estimated to be seven miles (11 km) long and about 2.4 miles (4 km) wide.

Professional meteorite hunter Robert Ward searching the Creston, California, hills for space rocks. Scientists who study meteorites often depend on professional hunters like Robert to be their feet—and eyes—on the ground.

Prescott, Arizona, and travel around the globe to collect these precious space rocks.

Meteorite hunters search the area under and around recent fireballs as quickly as possible—usually on foot. Sometimes it's a race against rain, snow, dust, or plant growth, which will cover the meteorites or destroy them. "We need to get the meteorites out of the weather as fast as possible," says Marc. "Earth's water and oxygen will make them rust, and metal and other minerals will start to break down. The quicker you can

recover a meteorite, the more accurate picture you get of what the original asteroid was really like and where the meteorite might have come from."

On one hunt, Robert and his wife and fellow hunter, Anne Marie Ward, and Marc and his wife, Linda Welzenbach, a research scientist with the Planetary Science Institute, gathered

Research scientist Marc Fries on the hunt for the Creston meteorites. At one point, Marc says: "Come here, little meteorite. Let me find you and keep you from rusting away in the rain." He's joking—but only partly.

to search for meteorites from a fireball over Creston, California. Bundled up against the damp, foggy weather, they spread out and began crisscrossing the undulating hills of golden grass, studying the ground.

It's a game of "One of These Things Is Not Like the Other." What looks different from all the other rocks around? What

Linda Welzenbach and Marc Fries discuss the composition of a rock they found in the Creston, California, hills while searching for meteorites.

doesn't fit in? What might have come from outer space? Fallen meteorites are often dull, blackened rocks that look like they are coated with charcoal. "As we're searching, we know there are meteorites next to us somewhere," says Robert. "That's the fun of it. It's a treasure hunt."

Eventually, Robert spots a very round and shallow pit with no piles of dirt surrounding it. "A meteorite could have hit here and rolled or bounced out," he says. He crisscrosses the area more slowly, looking three or four feet ahead as he goes.

Linda finds something promising under a cluster of trees. She picks up a round object with a blackened outer layer that looks like a meteorite fusion crust. She palms the item lightly

THE BEST HUNTING IN THE WORLD

The most promising place on the planet to find meteorites is also one of the coldest and hardest to get to: the Antarctic. Glacial-ice movement concentrates meteorites that have fallen over tens of thousands of years into areas the size of the Creston strewn field. Also, the dark meteorites stand out starkly against the pale blue ice.

Linda Welzenbach (right) and Andy Caldwell with a new meteorite find in the Antarctic.

Since 1976, scientists with the U.S. Antarctic Meteorite Program have found more than twenty thousand meteorites. Linda Welzenbach has searched there twice, camping on blue ice along the Transantarctic Mountainss in −70°F (−57°C) temperatures. She and her colleagues found 603 meteorites the first time and 855 the second. Each find is photographed, described, and located by GPS. The meteorites are shipped frozen to NASA's Johnson Space Center in Houston and eventually stored in special cabinets at the Smithsonian. "We treat them as carefully as lunar rocks to protect all the information they may contain," says Linda.

and tosses it gently in the air. "This is way too round for a meteorite," says Linda, who has handled many meteorites as a curator for the Smithsonian Institution in Washington, D.C. "It's also really lightweight, and meteorites are usually quite dense." She points to a tree. "It's probably just a gall from that live oak."

The team hunts all day, picking up rocks and discarding them. Too flat. Too lightweight. Too shiny. Too round.

Hunts, Robert says, are one part luck, two parts science, and three parts hard work. He and Anne Marie comb the Creston hills for three weeks. One morning, they climb out of the truck and there, scattered on the road around a fence post, are rock fragments with what looks like a black fusion crust and a light gray interior. These appear to be pieces of a meteorite that smashed into the fence post after plummeting down from space. But the Wards want to determine the exact type of meteorite.

Meteorite hunters depend on scientists like Dolores Hill of the Lunar and Planetary Laboratory at the University of Arizona to classify potential meteorites. To Dolores, meteorites are puzzle pieces falling from space. They have already helped answer important questions, such as, What are asteroids made of? (Varying combinations of carbon, silicate rock, and metals such as iron-nickel.) And what kind and size of asteroid are most likely to survive the trip through the atmosphere? (Larger, more metallic, and less fractured asteroids, which pose the biggest danger.)

METEOR-WRONGS

METEORITES

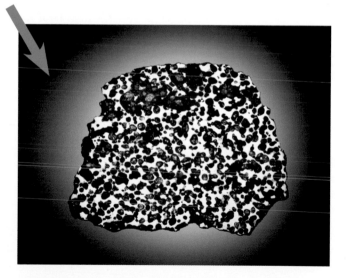

Robert Ward found this stony meteorite after a witnessed fall in the mountains of Nevada. Stony meteorites are the most common type, accounting for more than 90 percent of meteorite falls. Scientists think they come from the remnants of minor planets and asteroids left over after the formation of the solar system.

He acquired this iron meteorite from a 1947 fireball witnessed in Russia. Fewer than 5 percent of meteorites found on Earth are iron; they originate from the cores of long-gone planets, dwarf planets, and large asteroids. Iron asteroids are perhaps the most dangerous as their strength and density increase the chances that they can power through our atmosphere and smash into the ground.

Robert found this gorgeous stony-iron meteorite in Canada. Only 2 percent of meteorites found on Earth feature this even mix of stone and metal (nickel-iron). Scientists think these rocks come from the boundary between the core and the mantle of space objects such as ancient planets and asteroids. The mix of minerals makes some stony-iron meteorites the most beautiful space rocks to behold.

To determine if a rock is really a meteorite, Dolores first checks for a fusion crust—a thin black melted coating that might look brownish if the rock has been weathered. She also looks for thumbprint-like indentations, which often form during a high-speed descent.

Then she feels the weight of the rock. Is it heavier than it looks? Meteorites are generally denser than Earth rocks.

Does the rock attract a magnet? Most meteorites contain some metal—and iron meteorites will grab a magnet tightly. But not all rocks that attract magnets are meteorites and not all meteorites attract a magnet.

So Dolores chips off a piece or slices the rock open with a diamond-studded saw. A dull black fusion crust with a different color of stone or metal inside means she might really have a meteorite in her hands.

The charcoal-like fusion crust and dull, speckled gray interior of the Wards' find immediately identifies it as a stony meteorite with chondrules (mineral grains) known as an "ordinary chondrite."

To confirm that the rock is a meteorite and determine its composition, Dolores places a thin slice of the rock into the lab's million-dollar electron microprobe. The electron beam zaps each tiny spot to determine its elements and mineral composition. "The composition begins to give us a picture of the asteroid's early formation, what collisions it experienced, what part of the asteroid the fragment came from, and maybe even

Dolores Hill gets a sense of the amount of metal in a rock by checking whether a magnet is attracted to it.

Dolores holds a thin section of a meteorite ready to view with a microscope or microprobe.

where in the solar system the meteorite originated: the asteroid belt? Vesta? The moon? Mars?" says Dolores.

The origin of the Wards' Creston meteorite remains a mystery. The composition seems similar to that of a large near-Earth asteroid called Eros, which was visited by a spacecraft in 2000-2001. Astronomers worry that gravitational interactions may nudge Eros into a dangerous Earth-crossing orbit sometime in the next two million years. If Eros is headed our way, we will be glad to have an actual sample of the rock that could hit us.

That's because scientists who study asteroids know that boulders from space can leave behind something much larger than meteorites. They can leave behind giant scars on the land.

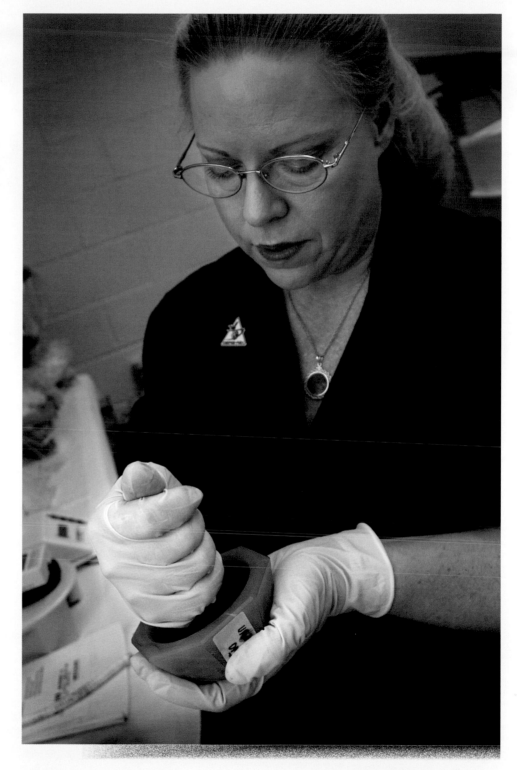

Using a mortar and pestle, Dolores grinds rock. Dust can be used to determine whether or not a rock sample is a meteorite and, if so, what kind.

Meteor Crater from the rim.

Chapter Three

BLAST FROM THE PAST

The long plateau of sagebrush and desert grasses east of Flagstaff, Arizona, is flat, brown, and dry for miles. From a distance it's easy to miss the massive hole in the ground. The crater is deep, 550 feet (168 m)—large enough to hide a sixty-story skyscraper. And the crater is wide, 2.3 miles (3.7 km) around, big enough to encircle the downtown area of most cities.

For many years, people assumed the crater was caused by a volcanic eruption. Then iron meteorite fragments were discovered all around it. "But people just couldn't wrap their heads around the idea that a huge asteroid could soar in from outer space, hit the Earth, and cause this much destruction," says Da-

vid Kring, a senior scientist at the Lunar and Planetary Institute in Houston, Texas. Evidence eventually piled up proving that the hole—now called Meteor Crater—was blasted out by an asteroid impact roughly fifty thousand years ago.

For more than a decade, David has been hiking through this rubble and climbing carefully down the sheer cliffs to read from the rocks the story of the massive destruction that happened here. "From the study of impact craters there's a lot we can learn about asteroids and the dangers they pose," says David. "There is nothing hypothetical about it. Meteor Crater, Chelyabinsk, and other events tell us conclusively what asteroids can do."

David has probably walked more of Meteor Crater than anyone else in the world. "I'm exploring the threshold of what size and type of asteroid forms a crater," he explains, "what size impact causes local, citywide, regional, and global consequences—what would destroy a modern city versus what would cause mass global extinctions."

With his long, lean build, khaki pants, army-green shirt, and brown hiking boots, David could pass for a park ranger. But the rock hammer he holds in his right hand, like an extension of his arm, pegs him as a geologist. "The hammer, magnifying glass, and camera are the essential tools of a geologist," says David. "But the most powerful tool is the human eye. It is our ability to observe closely and to imagine what happened in three dimensions that allows us to recreate what happened here."

Standing on the rim of Meteor Crater, David tells the story that he and his colleagues have been able to piece together: Fifty thousand years ago, this area was wetter and cooler, with giant mammoths roaming the green plateau, munching on grass, sedges, and small shrubs. Stubbier, muscular mastodons kept mostly to the forest, chomping on juniper and pinion trees. Ground sloths, with their blunt noses, powerful jaws, and clawed limbs, scooted between both areas, nibbling on yucca, agave, globe mallow, and Mormon tea plants.

Then one day, as they munched unconcerned, a huge, heavy iron rock, as wide as a basketball court, screamed toward Earth at a speed of roughly forty thousand miles (64,374 km) per hour, or fifty times the speed of sound. As the asteroid hit the atmos-

David Kring describes, using many gestures, what he thinks happened when an asteroid struck outside of Flagstaff, Arizona, fifty thousand years ago. "Geology is really about seeing and thinking in 3D," he says. "You have to imagine what is going on below the surface and see moving pictures in your head of how things might have changed over time."

18

The normal order of the colors of rock in this area—rust red on top, yellow in the middle, and gray on the bottom—were completely reversed in the rubble of rock on the rim of Meteor Crater, which goes from gray on top to yellow and then red. "We think that the shock wave from an asteroid impact uplifted the crater wall and flipped it upside down with a giant WHUMPF, forming the rim," says David, standing on the overturned red Moenkopi rock layer.

phere, the friction heated the front of the cold rock and it glowed with a blinding light. But the friction didn't slow this massive rock down very much. It plowed into the ground at almost full speed, releasing an immense explosion.

The asteroid penetrated more than a hundred feet (30 m) into the ground, compressing the rock beneath it. The back half burst into tiny fragments that launched skyward and rained down upon the land for miles.

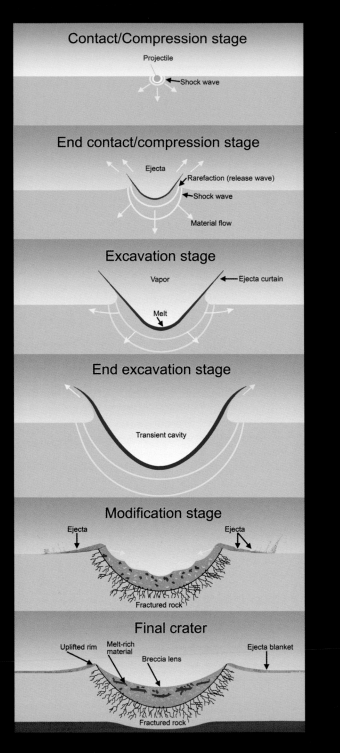

Contact/Compression stage
Projectile
Shock wave

End contact/compression stage
Ejecta
Rarefaction (release wave)
Shock wave
Material flow

Excavation stage
Vapor
Ejecta curtain
Melt

End excavation stage
Transient cavity

Modification stage
Ejecta
Ejecta
Fractured rock

Final crater
Uplifted rim
Melt-rich material
Breccia lens
Ejecta blanket
Fractured rock

But that was just the beginning. The impact shot powerful shock waves in all directions that massively compressed the ground in a 2.3 mile (3.7 kilometer) circle and sent rock exploding skyward. Huge boulders and rubble from deep in the ground careened though the dust-choked air in all directions at speeds up to 228 miles (366 km) per hour, as fast as a racecar, pummeling the terrain for miles. Even traveling at those speeds, it took a full minute for all the debris to land.

The demolished asteroid left behind a crater three-quarters of a mile (1.2 km) wide. But the destruction the asteroid wrought reached much farther—up to seven miles away. If a

Gray Coconino sandstone was the deepest layer blasted by the asteroid's shock wave. In fact, the shock was so powerful that it crushed some of this sandstone, altering its composition and turning it into this bright white floury rock. Crushed, or "shocked," sandstone is unique to impact craters—hard evidence that an asteroid has struck.

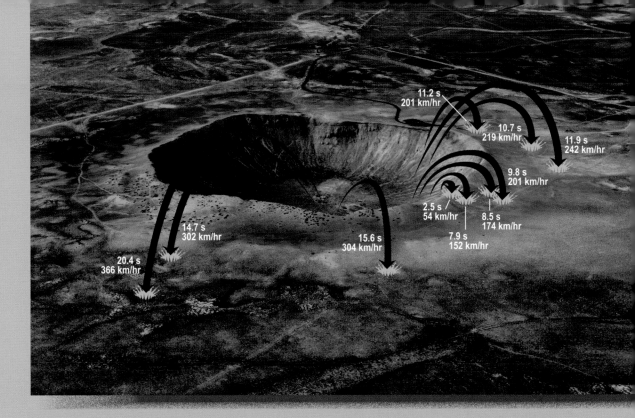

11.2 s
201 km/hr

10.7 s
219 km/hr

11.9 s
242 km/hr

9.8 s
201 km/hr

2.5 s /
54 km/hr

8.5 s
174 km/hr

14.7 s
302 km/hr

15.6 s
304 km/hr

7.9 s
152 km/hr

20.4 s
366 km/hr

David's graduate students measured the locations of several large boulders around Meteor Crater and calculated how fast boulders inside the crater had rocketed through the sky after the asteroid hit and how long before they landed outside the crater rim. One large rock hit at a speed of about 230 miles (370 km) per hour, landing about a third of a mile (.5 km) beyond the crater rim.

medium-size city such as Kansas City had been in the asteroid's path, it would have been wiped off the map completely.

David is working to develop an even more detailed understanding of what happened during the impact. He and his students have spent weeks, months, even years mapping how a layer of gray sandstone, called Coconino, is distributed in the vast plateau outside the crater. "Because Coconino comes from the deepest part of the target rock, more energy would be needed to move it," says David. "The distribution of the Coconino may tell us something about how energy was distributed in the explosion."

"Ultimately, we want to be able to say that an asteroid of this size, this composition, coming in at this angle will cause this amount of damage," says David. "It's the only way we can begin to address the hazard posed by something coming at us from outer space."

David also has a mystery to solve, something odd he noticed in the rock layers on the south rim of the crater. In the bedrock, a yellow layer called Kaibab limestone is more than 260 feet (80 m) thick. But on the south rim of the crater where the rock was thrown during the impact, the yellow Kaibab layer is thin, just four and half feet (1.4 m).

"That's eighty meters of Kaibab just missing!" he exclaims. "Where did it go?"

David studied the crater and the debris (ejecta) area around it for years, pondering this question. "I came up with this idea that maybe something in the bedrock structure made the Kaibab squirt through the other two layers," David says. He turns his back to the crater and points toward the flat plateau in the distance. "If that were true, I hypothesized that we would find loads of Kaibab way out there."

So he walked the dry, dusty plain outside the south rim of the crater under the hot desert sun, crisscrossing a wide area, observing, and taking measurements of the depth of the Kaibab deposits. His initial finding? "I think it is there," he says. He won't know for sure until he rallies a group of graduate students to thoroughly map the area. But his findings are promising enough that he wants to venture into the crater to figure out what caused all that Kaibab to shoot so far in one direction. Was there something about the way the underground rock was shaped that could have directed the energy of the impact that way?

David demonstrates how a bowl-shaped bedrock structure could have funneled massive amounts of Kaibab rock far out of the crater when the asteroid hit.

WHAT TO CARRY INTO A CRATER

When working at Meteor Crater and other impact sites, David Kring carries a wide range of supplies in his backpack:

A radio, to keep in touch with officials at Meteor Crater and with graduate students and colleagues. Also, he can call for help if needed.

A camera. "All geologists are photographers," says David. "Photos help us see and remember the rocks so we can make sense of the data later."

Lots of water, especially when working in the desert.

Brunton Compass, to help him figure out the orientation of a rock.

Notebook and pen, to write about what he sees and imagines, so he doesn't forget.

Gloves, to handle sharp rocks.

Sunscreen, to protect his skin from the blazing hot desert sun.

Energy bars, to keep him going as he explores and studies the crater.

Fifty-foot (15 m) tape measure, to take accurate measurements of the lengths of features such as outcrops and thrown boulders.

Knife, for cutting rope—and rock!

A Leatherman, which has multiple tools that might come in handy.

Flagging tape, to mark an area he wants to study more closely.

Calipers, to take accurate measurements of small rocks.

Magnifying lens, to see the grains of a rock up close.

Plastic zip-top bags, for rock and dust samples.

Sharpies, to label plastic bags with sample numbers and to make note of tests he might want to conduct with that sample, such as "Look at the olivine."

First-aid kit with a reflective emergency blanket for warmth, a whistle to call for help, a small compass so he knows the direction he's headed, and a signal mirror to flash toward a plane or other rescue party if needed.

Stopping to take notes as he goes, David heads down the steep slopes of Meteor Crater.

David measures the angle of an outcrop with a Brunton Compass to test his theory that the bedrock was bowl-shaped when the asteroid struck.

"We have to take advantage of all the information about asteroids that an impact site provides us," says David. "Because heaven forbid something is headed toward us and we don't really understand what it can do. It's not an experiment I want to play out in real time on Earth."

Starting out along a dusty path, David peers down the steep cliff slopes searching for a safe way into the crater. A cold breeze sends a chill. He steps off the trail and heads immediately down the slope, weaving through the brush and loose rock to a spot below a small outcrop of Kaibab. The sheer cliff drops five hundred feet (150 m) below.

David places his feet firmly on solid rocks and pulls his yellow field book from his thigh pocket. After gazing around slowly and studying the rock outcrop, he begins taking notes, describing in detail where he is and what he plans to do: he's

going to walk along the narrow edge of a steep cliff and take readings of the orientation of the rocks, the way the bedrock faces. Perhaps the angle of the rocks will explain the path that the Kaibab layer took during impact.

After considering an outcrop a few feet away, David edges toward it, working his way around the dried skeletons of juniper trees. Leaning into the hill, he searches for the biggest, most secure rock to hold his weight. Out comes the Brunton Compass, which he opens and lays on the upper edge of the rock. Head bent over his tool and his notebook, he takes a reading.

"If the bedrocks form a bowl shape here, which is what I think they do, that will show up in the data, with the rocks on one side of the bowl dipping one way and the rocks on the other side dipping the other way," says David.

David tries to take another reading of another outcrop,

David takes detailed notes of his measurements and observations in his field journal to help him understand exactly what happened at Meteor Crater when the asteroid hit.

but the edge is so jagged he can't get the compass to lie flat. So he slips his hardcover notebook between the rock and the compass. "This way we can at least get the average angle," he explains.

He continues his journey across the sheer cliff, no longer on firm outcrops. The slope has turned to treacherous rubble. Rocks slide, clinking and clattering, toward him. David ducks his head and shoulders under an outcrop, and the rocks shoot by him, crashing toward the crater floor. He decides he has enough data on this side of the bowl. He'll come back another day to brave the other side.

Settled on a boulder on the crater rim, David reviews his notes. For now, his data seem to support his theory. All of the eight outcrops where he measured point to the southwest with a five- to twenty-five-degree tilt, like one side of a bowl. For

now, it seems like the structure of the bedrock may have acted like a funnel, channeling the destructive power of the asteroid impact.

"I really feel like a pioneer, discovering something no one has ever discovered before," David says. "And it's important work, because what I learn could ultimately affect millions of people's lives if there is an asteroid headed for Earth—and there probably is."

If the past is any indication, we may have more to fear than the destructive force David has encountered at Meteor Crater. Asteroid impacts have shaped our planet in ways we can hardly imagine.

When taking students to the crater for the first time, David likes to pull over at the turn-off from Highway 40, about six miles (10 km) from the crater. He asks them to describe what they would have seen of the impact if they had been on this spot fifty thousand years ago. After they finish their vivid descriptions, he drops the bomb. "You wouldn't have seen anything because you'd be dead."

No firsthand representations of dinosaurs are available because they went extinct sixty-five million years ago. Based on bone and fossil records, scientists create drawings and models of the creatures, such as the Tyrannosaurus rex pictured here. Theories about what the dinosaurs actually looked like change as our knowledge increases.

Chapter Four

THE DEATH OF THE DINOS

David Kring is one of the key scientists responsible for solving one of the greatest scientific mysteries of the twentieth century. Roughly sixty-five million years ago, the dinosaurs suddenly and mysteriously went extinct. No one knew why.

In 1980, father and son team Luis and Walter Alvarez pro-

As a child in Indiana, David Kring collected rocks, hunted fossils, and watched the *Apollo II* landing. "Me and all my friends wanted to do that," he says. To this day he is captivated by geology, ancient history, and space.

posed a revolutionary theory: an asteroid did the dinosaurs in. The scientists had been studying the composition of a layer of sixty-five-million-year-old rock, called the K-T boundary (Cretaceous-Tertiary), because it marked the transition from the dino to post-dino eras. They found that in several places around the world, the layer contained iridium, a metal rare on Earth's surface but plentiful in asteroids. They proposed that a massive fiery asteroid roughly six miles (10 km) wide smashed into Earth, sending iridium around the globe and the dinosaurs to their deaths.

David was a student at Indiana University when their theory was published. "The paper lit the world on fire," he says. "A professor called a meeting of the entire geology department to discuss it."

The Alvarezes predicted that the asteroid would have made a crater 100 to 125 miles (150–200 km) wide. "Everyone started looking," says David. People studied the distribution of iridium around the globe and suggested Iceland and India as possible locations. "But there was no evidence that these areas held the missing crater," says David. "The science was stalled." For years.

Walter Alvarez became frustrated, disappointed—even embarrassed. "Many of us were thinking we would never find it," he said in an interview.

In the late 1980s, David and his colleagues changed tactics. They realized that a massive asteroid impact would throw vast amounts of material all around it. Maybe looking at the

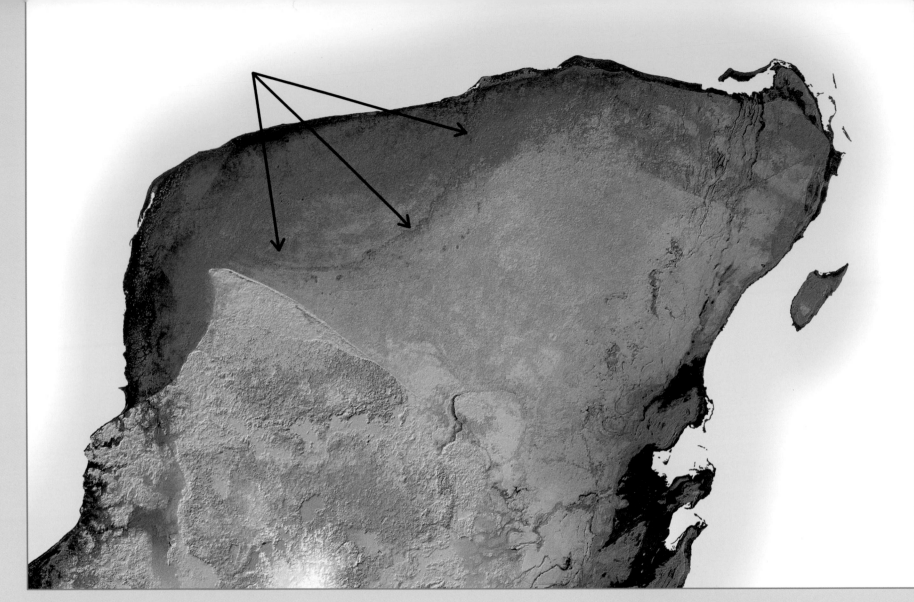

In this map of the Yucatan Peninsula in Mexico, a dark green curve shows the location of part of the rim of the Chicxulub crater. The rest of the crater is under water.

thickness of the material—called the ejecta—would draw a bull's-eye around the crater.

David traveled to Haiti, where possible evidence of ejecta had been found: small glassy beads that could have been from a volcano—or an asteroid impact. David, his guide, and a student, Alan Hildebrand, dug into the mountainside with shovels and pickaxes to reach rock untouched by tropical weather. Then they painstakingly took samples of each layer.

The work was hard—and made more dangerous by a military coup brewing in the country. David heard gunfire at night and saw new bullet holes in walls in the morning. "It was bad," he says. But he didn't want to leave. "We were peeling away the record of what happened, very delicately, one layer at a time."

David lugged a white canvas bag full of his samples onto a plane and back to his lab. There he and his colleagues found three important clues: iridium that matched the samples found in other places; glass beads, or tektite, which are caused by molten rock sprayed from an impact; and shocked quartz that had been altered by the pressure and heat of an impact.

The thickness of the K-T boundary layer, more than 1.5 feet (.5 m) in places, suggested that the impact crater was somewhere in the Gulf of Mexico or possibly in the Caribbean.

Some geologists focused on an area off the coast of Venezuela. But David and his colleagues thought a large 110-mile-wide (180 km) depression buried a half mile (800 m) deep under the Yucatan peninsula in Mexico seemed more promising.

The crater, named Chicxulub after a nearby town, was half under the Gulf of Mexico, half on land, and completely buried under hundreds of feet of sediment. The depression had been discovered by an oil company whose engineers' gravity and magnetic measurements mapped the crater. Scientists concluded that the crater was likely created by a volcanic eruption. But

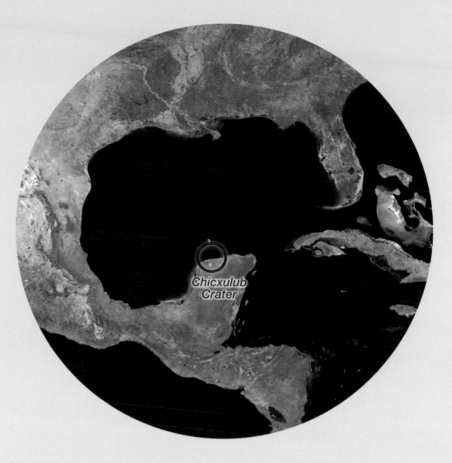

David knew that impact craters are often mistaken for volcanic craters.

In 1990, David, Alan, and their colleague William Boynton asked scientists who had worked with the oil company if they could look at their rock samples. The scientists handed over two thumb-size rock fragments taken from about three-quarters of a mile (1,200 m) below the surface. One was multicolored, with fragments of older rock that had been broken and recombined. The other was dark green. "I was so excited when I saw them," David says. "I had a strong feeling that these were impact rocks."

THE EVIDENCE

When an asteroid strikes, it can melt the rock it hits. Molten droplets thrown from the crater can cool into these glassy beads. David Kring found a thick layer of these beads in the K-T boundary in Haiti, suggesting that the crater from the asteroid impact that killed the dinosaurs was somewhere in that region.

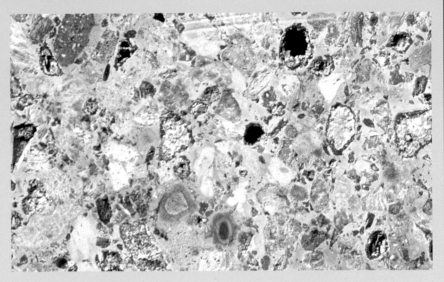

When David studied a borehole sample taken from a crater in Mexico, he discovered that this contains shocked quartz, which can be made by only one thing: an asteroid impact. Later he matched the compositions of rocks from the Chicxulub crater with the glass beads found in Haiti in the K-T boundary layer. These discoveries proved that the dinosaurs were killed by an asteroid strike at Chicxulub.

David cut paper-thin sections of the rocks, mounted them on glass, and polished them until light could pass through. Then he put them under his microscope.

"I immediately saw shocked quartz—layers of quartz, then layers of glass with the same composition, then layers of quartz, then glass," says David. "Shocked quartz is absolutely diagnostic of an impact. The impact destroys the structure of the quartz while keeping its composition. No other geological process creates shocked quartz, including volcanic eruptions."

He also found that the dark green rock was a melted mix of the rock from the region, including limestone and granite. "It was an absolutely unique composition," says David. Again, not something that comes from volcanoes.

To confirm when the asteroid strike occurred, David's colleagues studied radioactive elements in the sample to see how much they had broken down. This radiometric dating placed the time of the crater formation at 64.98 million years ago, plus or minus fifty thousand years—just when the dinosaurs disappeared.

OTHER BIG HITS

Other massive asteroids have struck Earth without causing massive extinctions. About 35 million years ago, an asteroid five to eight miles (8–13 km) wide vaporized above what is now the Chesapeake Bay in Maryland. The asteroid left a fifty-six-mile-wide (90 km) crater twice the size of Rhode Island and as deep as the Grand Canyon.

Around the same time an asteroid three to five miles (5–8 km) wide blew out a twenty-mile wide (32 km) crater at Popigai in Siberia, Russia. The Popigai crater has a silver—or rather sparkling—lining, so to speak. Graphite shocked by the impact created the world's largest diamond deposit.

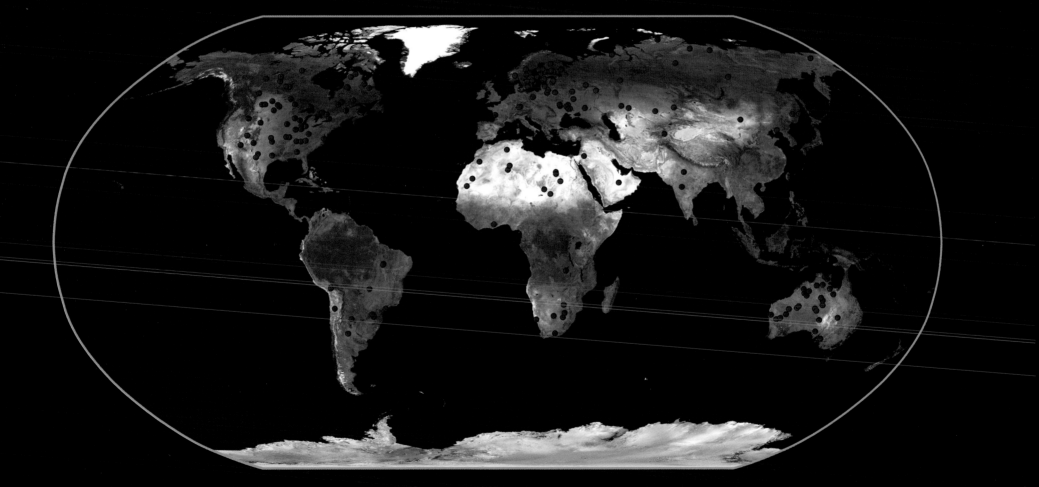

Red dots show the locations of the 183 asteroid impact craters that have been discovered on Earth. Many more asteroids have struck Earth, but their craters have been destroyed by erosion and other geologic processes.

David announced the findings at a meeting at NASA's Johnson Space Center in Houston. Excitement filled the room but some questions remained. Why was material from the impact—such as quartz—distributed so unevenly across the planet, with the largest chunks found in North America? And why were there more extinctions in North America than in South America?

Scientists surmised that the asteroid skidded in from the southeast and hurled debris to the northwest and skyward. They tested the theory by shooting large objects at flat rock at a shallow angle using high-speed guns. The result: a crater just like Chicxulub.

"Once we found the location, we began to recreate the event," David says. "We knew exactly where it hit, what type of rock it hit, how deep the water was. We could do some serious calculations to figure out what really happened." So what did David and his colleagues piece together?

Roughly sixty-five million years ago, a huge rock—six miles (10 km) wide—screamed toward the planet at more than forty times the speed of sound. The asteroid was so large— bigger than Mount Everest—that when one end of the rock reached the surface, the other side was still up in the sky at the cruising altitude of airplanes.

The asteroid smashed into a shallow sea and penetrated six miles (10 km) into the seabed. The energy released was roughly a thousand times the energy contained in all existing nuclear weapons. The giant *BOOM!* of the impact was probably heard everywhere on Earth. Huge earthquakes, of magnitude 11 or greater, shook the planet. Massive tsunamis—160 to 1,000 feet (50–300 m) high—pummeled the Gulf of Mexico, stripping huge areas bare of vegetation and animal life.

Shock waves produced high-velocity winds, as high as one thousand miles an hour, which scoured the land of all plants, animals, and soil for a thousand miles (1,500 km) in all directions. A pulse of heat measuring 18,000°F (10,000°C) torched the ground as far as 2,500 miles (4,000 km) away—almost the same distance as between the east and west coasts of the United States.

An artist's concept of the Chicxulub asteroid hitting Earth in the time of dinosaurs.

ONE WORLD ENDS,
ANOTHER BEGINS

"There is another way to look at Chicxulub," says David. "It is the cradle of humanity. It changed the biological evolution of the planet Earth, which opened the way for the evolution of mammals and eventually *Homo sapiens*."

Indeed, some scientists think early asteroid impacts may have been responsible for the development of life itself. "Microbial life thrives in hydrothermal [hot water] environments," David says. "The most primitive life forms may have been generated in subsurface hydrothermal environments created in the wake of destructive asteroid impacts four billion years ago. Asteroids might have provided the habitat for the origin and early evolution of life."

The impact disintegrated the Earth's crust, throwing up a cascade of rocky debris that buried the surrounding landscape up to a half mile (800 m) deep, and launching a fiery spray of molten rock that landed throughout the Western Hemisphere. The impact also sent a hot plume of vaporized rock into space, where it wrapped around the planet. Gravity pulled the scorching material back through the atmosphere at speeds up to twenty-five thousand miles (40,000 km) an hour. The roaring debris heated the atmosphere to several hundred degrees, igniting wildfires in the United States and additional pockets around the globe. It didn't matter whether the material rained down on

desert or swamp—the hot temperatures drove moisture from everything and set it all ablaze.

Soot and dust choked out the sunlight. "Some models suggest that if you were there, you couldn't see your hand in front of your face for six months," says David. This darkness might have been the most deadly environmental consequence. Plants that required sun for photosynthesis died. The base of the marine food chain, plankton, perished from lack of sunlight. Species that ate those plants died and so on up the food chain. Even in areas untouched by the wildfires, such as the oceans, life withered.

The fires also produced toxic gases that damaged the ozone layer, which protects the earth from radiation. When the ash finally fell out of the sky over the next few months, it fell with acid rain that poisoned water and soil almost everywhere.

After about five years of global winter, the gases created a greenhouse effect, trapping heat inside the atmosphere and warming the planet. "We don't know how hot and for how long," says David.

After the roar of the fires burned down, the world would have been hushed—with only the lonely sounds of wind, water, and rain. Dinosaurs were not the only creatures to be decimated. More than 75 percent of plant and animals species went extinct.

"The world took three to four million years to recover," says David. "And life never returned to the way it was."

Imagine if an asteroid strike of this magnitude happened

In 1908, an asteroid about 120 feet (37 m) long entered the atmosphere at more than 33,000 miles (53,000 km) per hour, heating the air to almost 45,000°F (25,000°C). The asteroid detonated in the sky above Tunguska, Siberia, scorching and plowing down 80 million trees. On average a Tunguska-size asteroid will reach Earth once every three hundred years.

today. Could it? Are there asteroids as big as this one hurtling though our solar system? Knowing is a matter of national and international security. So in 1992, the U.S. Congress directed NASA to locate at least 90 percent of the near-Earth asteroids larger than .62 miles (1 km) across. Astronomers have found almost all (95 percent) of these behemoths, which are big enough to destroy whole continents—and life on Earth as we know it. Thankfully, none are on a collision course with our planet.

But scientists estimate that another 5 percent are still to be discovered. And soaring out in our solar system are an estimated thirteen to twenty thousand asteroids big enough to vaporize a whole city. Astronomers have found only about one in ten of these. And while scientists have discovered and tracked about a thousand asteroids similar in size to the Chelyabinsk asteroid that burst over Russia a few years ago, there are millions more they have not yet found.

The fact is, we don't really know when the next dangerous asteroid will strike. For a long time, scientists thought an asteroid strike like the one that exploded above Chelyabinsk happened only about once every 150 years. But new evidence suggests they might be much more frequent—perhaps every few decades. And the threat of larger strikes is tiny—but constant. "We know two things for sure," says David. "Big asteroid strikes are exceedingly rare—but it's also true that they could happen any time."

That's why we need to find them first.

Chapter Five

ASTEROID HUNT!

T he Catalina Sky Survey—home base for some of the world's best asteroid hunters—sits at the top of Arizona's Mount Lemmon at 9,157 feet (2,791 m). A chainlink fence around the compound holds a large sign: NO HEADLIGHTS. Nothing must interfere with the important work that happens here from sunset to sunrise: scouring the solar system for asteroids whose orbits might bring them into a collision course with Earth.

The biggest of the survey's three telescopes, the sixty-inch (1.5 m) instrument that finds the majority of the asteroids, sits

(Far left) Catalina Sky Survey principal investigator Eric Christensen opens the largest of the asteroid survey's three telescopes to prepare it for a night of asteroid hunting.

(Center) The view of the summit of Mount Lemmon from Catalina's sixty-inch (1.5 m) telescope. Some of the telescopes are run remotely from locations around the globe.

inside a large white dome, like a huge silo. Eric Christensen, the principal investigator for Catalina, unlocks the door and flicks on the lights—eerie red lights. Any white light shining out of the dome opening could impede the view of other telescopes on the mountain.

Eric pushes a button. With a loud clatter, a pulley system lowers a wide gray metal panel of the dome, like a drawbridge

All the buildings on Mount Lemmon with doors or windows to the outside are equipped with red lights so white light won't interfere with the telescopes' ability to detect faint light in the solar system.

DAY SLEEPERS
DO NOT DISTURB
BEFORE 1:00 P.M.

All the asteroid search work at Catalina and other sky surveys happens at night. Observers and researchers sleep during the day in quiet, darkened dormitories.

of a castle. A frigid wind roars in. Another button slides the upper panel open, like a long garage door. Heavy gusts blow at Eric's beard. "Not good," Eric says. "We might need to raise the lower shutter to act as a wind shield." He adjusts the opening to minimize the wind.

"Now the telescope," he says. He presses another button and four triangular black flaps on the telescope unfurl like the petals of a flower, opening a giant mirror to the sky. The mirror will gather all the light it can from the night sky and send it to the wide-angle camera, which will record objects moving across the sky.

"At any given moment, there are probably a few dozen unknown near-Earth asteroids within range of our telescopes," says Eric. But will they find them?

Asteroid hunters—called observers—work from sunset to sunrise, in this case from about 6:30 p.m. to 6:30 a.m. The process—point the telescope, shoot pictures, review pictures to find moving objects, report potential asteroids—is the same every night and is repeated over and over throughout the night. But where to search changes each night and as the night progresses.

Eric has been obsessed with astronomy since he was twelve years old, when he saved his allowance to buy a subscription to an astronomy magazine. Then he began saving for a telescope. "It was a big purchase for a kid," Eric says. "I paid half and my parents paid half." He landed summer jobs at a local observatory, doing maintenance and painting. "I love being around ob-

Eric Christensen spends most of his night of asteroid hunting in front of four large computer monitors that help him direct the sixty-inch (1.5 m) telescope and review the photos it takes.

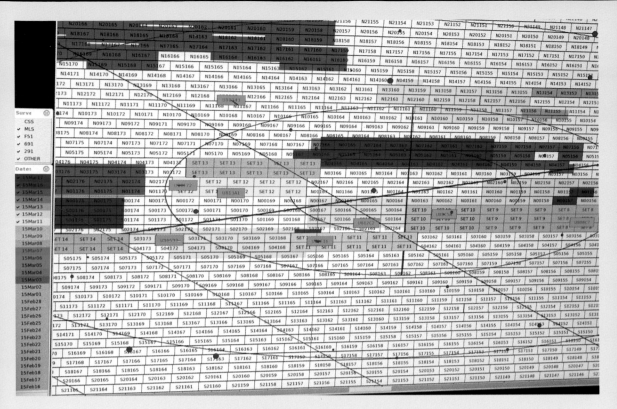

This close-up of one of Eric's computer monitors shows how asteroid hunters see what parts of the sky have been searched recently (red, orange, and yellow areas) and how they mark sections of the sky for the telescope to photograph (labeled by set number).

servatories, around the telescopes, all the tinkering and engineering that happens," he says. Since graduating from college, he has continued working at observatories, doing maintenance for a few years and later hunting asteroids full time.

Eric settles into an office chair in front of four large monitors in a small, warm room adjacent to the telescope. He turns his attention to the screen that displays a map of the night sky, divided into small rectangles like Lego bricks. Most of the rectangles are light gray, which means that no one has observed that area of the sky recently. Red, orange, and yellow bricks mark areas that have been observed in the last few days, with red being searched most recently.

OTHER ASTEROID SURVEYS

Catalina Sky Survey is not the only group searching for asteroids. Asteroid hunters can also be found at these surveys:

Lincoln Near-Earth Asteroid Research (LINEAR) focuses on finding big asteroids and has been responsible for discovering many of the behemoths—three thousand feet (1 km) or bigger. The survey has found more than 2,400 near-Earth objects (NEOs).

Panoramic Survey Telescope and Rapid Response System (Pan-STARRS) finds near-Earth asteroids from the top of Haleakala, the dormant volcano in Maui, Hawaii. Its wide-view telescope can search about one-sixth of the sky every month and holds the record for the number of asteroids discovered in one night: nineteen. The group plans to add another asteroid-searching telescope in the future.

Spacewatch on Kitt Peak in Arizona has transitioned from a successful asteroid hunting survey to more of a NEO follow-up program, leaving the bigger telescopes more time to find never-before-seen asteroids.

While observing at the sixty-inch (1.5 m) telescope of the Catalina Sky Survey, Eric Christensen discovered this near-Earth asteroid moving across the backdrop of stars. The asteroid is circled in each image. The asteroid is about sixty-six feet (20 m) across—about the size of the Chelyabinsk asteroid. Its orbit is similar in size and shape to Earth's orbit, and will bring the asteroid close to Earth frequently, with the next flyby in 2029.

An alarm sounds: *WEE-AH, WEE-AH.* The telescope is letting Eric know that the sun has set, the sky has darkened, and the time has come to search. He clicks on six gray bricks representing six small sections of the sky, low on the horizon to the west.

That low angle is a tough place to look because the telescope has to peer through a deep layer of moisture in the atmosphere. Also, objects there won't be fully lit by the sun— like a crescent moon. "Most likely we won't find anything here," says Eric. "But if we do, it would be very interesting." By interesting

he means possibly dangerous. That's because anything he finds would be very close to Earth. "Objects that spend a lot of time in near-Earth space are more likely to eventually collide with the planet," Eric says.

The dome grinds and groans as it spins its opening toward the target area. The telescope turns and lifts its camera to the sky. It takes a quick picture, moves to an adjacent spot and takes another picture, and so on, until it has taken a photo of all the sections Eric marked. Then the telescope repeats this exact process three more times. Automatically the computer scans through all the photos, noting objects that seem to be moving compared to the rest of the sky.

After about twenty minutes the computer has prepared the most promising photos for Eric's review. As powerful as the telescope, camera, and software are, the survey needs the human eye to confirm the finding of a real asteroid.

Eric leans toward the screen and peers at black photos scattered with white dots of different sizes. On each photo, one white dot has a circle around it. This is an object that the computer has flagged as a possible near-Earth asteroid because it seems to move relative to the more stable background of stars and planets. Eric flips through sets of four photos at what seems to be lightning speed. "We designed the software to be very sensitive to anything that might move position from photo to photo," says Eric. "That means we have to weed through a lot of false positives. But this way we'll be less likely to miss something important."

He flips through the whole set in about ten minutes. Nothing.

Eric continues like this for a few hours, directing the telescope to different parts of the sky. The dome and telescope groan as they move, like a train rumbling by every few minutes.

Eric reviews more and more photos—but finds nothing. He rubs his eyes. "You can get cross-eyed searching these photos all night," he says.

At 11 p.m., as Eric is whipping through sets of photos, he suddenly stops. "This object is potentially interesting," he says. He slowly toggles through the four photos and a white light clearly moves across the screen from lower left to upper right. "I'm going to report this one right away."

Professional observers and amateur astronomers all across the globe report suspected asteroids to the Minor Planet Center in Cambridge, Massachusetts. The center immediately lists them on its public website so others can track them. It's not enough to discover an asteroid. Astronomers have to establish its orbit to find out if the asteroid and the Earth orbit on the same plane, if their orbits cross, and if they may one day be on a collision course.

When scientists at the Minor Planet Center confirm an asteroid, they also calculate the rock's path for the next hundred years to estimate whether it poses a danger to our planet. More than six hundred asteroids are considered impact risks.

That doesn't mean more than six hundred asteroids are going to smash into Earth. Rather, this many objects could have orbits that cross the Earth's orbit. "Ninety-nine times out of a hundred, the longer we can track an object, the more we know about it, the less we have to worry," says Eric. "As we learn more, we rule out most possible impacts—and take the object off the list." But many, many asteroids stay on the list year after year. "If we lose them, we can't rule out the threat," he says.

The telescope Eric uses can only detect objects that are lit up by the sun and can see objects most clearly when they are at the opposite side of the sky from the sun. This is called being "in opposition," which happens around midnight. That prime searching time is approaching, and things start to get exciting.

Eric turns on some music to get in a groove. At one in the morning, he notices a weird streak that the computer didn't even highlight. "My gut tells me it's a NEO," he says. "And it's close." He decides to follow that one before reporting it. "When an object is this close, the key question is, is it geocentric, orbiting Earth like the moon, or heliocentric, orbiting the sun like a planet," he explains. "If it's orbiting Earth, we lose interest fast because it's probably a human-made satellite. But if it's orbiting the sun, well, it's very likely a very small, very close near-Earth asteroid."

Eric is trying to quickly review the rest of the photos when WEE-AH, WEE-AH—the telescope alarm sounds. The telescope needs to know where to search next. Eric picks some follow-ups and some new territory, and the telescope rumbles into place.

At 1:15, the follow-up photos on the weird streak come in. As Eric scans the four photos, the white dot seems to move across the screen to the beat of the blaring music. The object

This map of the solar system shows the orbits of the 1,400 Potentially Hazardous Asteroids (PHAs) that were discovered by 2013. Sky surveys have discovered many more since then.

is circling the sun. And it's about thirty-three feet (10 m) or so wide — the length of a school bus. "I want to observe this until I can't observe it anymore because this thing is quite close to us," Eric says.

To be considered a potentially hazardous asteroid (PHA) an object must have an orbit that brings it close to Earth, within 0.05 astronomical units (au) or about 4.6 million miles (7.5 million km). At roughly 435,000 miles (700,000 km), the object is definitely in range. But PHAs also have to be large — 460 feet (140 m) wide. And this one is likely a mere thirty-three feet (10 m).

Then Eric finds an object even closer, about halfway to the moon. "It's not going to hit, not on this pass anyway," he says. "But at less than lunar distance, if the orbit changes even slightly, it could bend into an impacting orbit." In fact, the most likely fate of this object is that it *will* hit Earth. "Give it a million years and I can almost guarantee it," he says.

At 2:17 a.m. Eric gets an email from the observer at one of the other Catalina telescopes who just found a really bright object. From its brightness and its distance from Earth, Eric estimates the size of this object at about sixty-five feet (20 m) — twice as big as the one he found earlier. This could pack a Chelyabinsk-size punch! Eric reports the asteroid right away so people around the globe can start tracking it.

LAST ALERT

What if an asteroid is in its final plunge toward Earth and all the sky surveys miss it? Two new telescopes in Hawaii, sensitive enough to detect a match flame more than three thousand miles (4,828 km) away, have recently begun keeping a close eye on near-Earth space for potentially hazardous asteroids (PHAs). Called the Asteroid Terrestrial-Impact Last Alert System (ATLAS), the telescopes can give a full day's warning for incoming Chelyabinsk-size asteroids and a week to three weeks for Meteor Crater–size city-smashers. Some notice is better than no notice. "That's enough time to evacuate the area of people, take measures to protect buildings and other infrastructure, and be alert to a tsunami danger generated by ocean impacts," says John Tonry, project director.

The ATLAS telescopes at the Haleakala Observatory being prepared to begin their search for asteroids whose orbits bring them in close range to Earth.

Clouds block all ground-based observatories from searching for asteroids.

Eric would like to track it too, but first he has to review photos from the fourteenth set of the night. And he has to keep the telescope busy searching new areas. Eric commands the telescope to search near the ecliptic, the plane of the solar system where the planets orbit. "Lots of asteroids also orbit here," Eric says, "so it's a productive place to search."

Then things start happening fast. At 2:34 a.m. something that looks like a long grain of rice bolts across the screen.

44

"Whoa!" Eric gasps. "We have to get a good follow-up on this one."

At 2:37: "Oh, we've got another streak. This one's going north. This guy will be long gone by tomorrow night; we've got to get another measurement." He reports it.

At 2:43, he leans toward the screen again. "Definitely a near-Earth asteroid," he says. "Definitely one we haven't seen before." He reports that one, too.

In all, Eric discovers an amazing ten new NEOs that night. When the Catalina Sky Survey first began, its asteroid hunters went months without finding any asteroids at all. In the 1990s, if they found three a month, they considered themselves lucky. These days, due to improved detectors, techniques, and software, they usually find at least three each night. Three doesn't seem like much, but in the last few years this has added up to about six hundred asteroid discoveries each year. Discoveries from all surveys combined is more than double that number—and growing.

The following night, Eric wants to scour parts of the sky that have not yet been searched and follow up on his new discoveries. But by 11 p.m. clouds start rolling in. Pointing the telescope between the clouds, he finds four more new objects. He's both excited and frustrated. "I need at least an hour more to follow up on these, to confirm them," he says. "And I know there are more out there . . ."

But the clouds have moved in and completely blocked Eric's view of the sky. The forecast calls for several days of clouds and rain. Eric has to shut down the search just as he's approaching the new moon, the darkest time of the month. Lightning threatens, so he unplugs everything to prevent damage to the delicate electronics. Then, reluctantly, Eric goes to bed.

In the next few hours, and in these next few nights, near-Earth asteroids will certainly soar within range of the Catalina telescope—unseen. More will whiz by undetected in the daylight hours. "We can't see through cloudy or stormy skies," Eric says. "We can't see anything that is coming from the direction of the sun. We can't see anything in daylight. This means that for every asteroid Catalina or the other surveys find, there are probably dozens around the size of the Chelyabinsk asteroid that we missed." And there is nothing to be done about it.

Or is there?

NASA's Wide-field Infrared Survey Explorer captured more than a hundred asteroids in this image. Asteroids show up as a series of dots that march across the sky. The asteroid at center left is called (2415) Ganesa.

Chapter Six

THE SEARCH FROM SPACE

Amy Mainzer and her colleagues know that searching for asteroids from space has some big advantages over searching from the ground. Amy is the principal investigator for the space mission NEOWISE (Near-Earth Object Wide Infrared Survey Explorer). Shaped like a thick barrel with a telescope and camera on one end, the unmanned NEOWISE spacecraft orbits Earth, taking photos of our solar system every eleven seconds. Unlike a ground telescope, it doesn't have to peer through the atmosphere. It doesn't have to wait for clear weather. It doesn't even have to wait for nightfall.

Amy Mainzer holds two coffee mugs, one hot and one cool. In the photo taken with visible light (top), there is no way to tell which mug is heated. In the infrared photo on the bottom, the heated mug glows more brightly (white on left), while the cold mug is black.

NEOWISE has another big advantage: It isn't looking for light. It's looking for heat.

Asteroids don't emit visible light like the stars and our sun. They reflect the sunlight. Like a white T-shirt, a light-colored asteroid reflects a lot of light. Dark-colored asteroids—like dark T-shirts—don't, so they are much harder to see against the dark background of space from regular ground telescopes.

Instead of relying on visible light, NEOWISE uses infrared light—wavelengths of light redder than the reddest red humans can see. "When you feel sun on your skin, you are feeling infrared light," Amy explains. Asteroids are warmed by the sun, so they glow extremely brightly at infrared wavelengths. In fact, darker asteroids absorb more of the sun's heat, so they shine even brighter at infrared wavelengths.

Between its launch in 2009 and 2011, the space telescope discovered lots of asteroids—*thirty-four thousand* asteroids, 134 of them orbiting near Earth.

There was a problem, though: the telescope had to stay cool in order to detect tiny amounts of heat far, far away in outer space. But the frozen hydrogen that cooled the instrument had run out.

NEOWISE was put into hibernation. Everything was powered down and turned off except what was needed to keep the spacecraft steady in its orbit. There it floated, dark and silent, around Earth.

The end of the mission was hard for the NEOWISE team members. "Having a spacecraft is like having a friend or a dog," says member Beth Fabinsky, who flew the spacecraft from mission control. "You see it every day, you get used to having it in your life. When you turn off the transmitter and you don't hear from it anymore, it's sad."

Then one day, Amy got a call from NASA. Public concerns over the threat of asteroid strikes were growing. NASA wanted her team to turn the spacecraft back on and continue the search.

"What?" Amy said. "Did I hear you right? Could you repeat that?"

She and her team went right to work writing a proposal to continue NEOWISE. "A lot of science is writing," Amy says. "You are always trying to convey what you've done or what you're hoping to do."

As the scientists prepared to extend the mission, they worried about how the spacecraft and telescope were doing. When they turned it back on, would everything work?

When the day came to restart, team members gathered around a blank screen. They transmitted to the spacecraft and waited to hear back. "Suddenly the screen filled with numbers and lines and we could see that it was alive," Beth says.

"Wahoooo!" the team cheered.

First, they pointed the telescope into deep space to cool it down. "The blackness of space is so cold that just by looking at it, the telescope loses heat," says Amy. On December 23, 2013, NEOWISE began work again, starting on a three-year mission

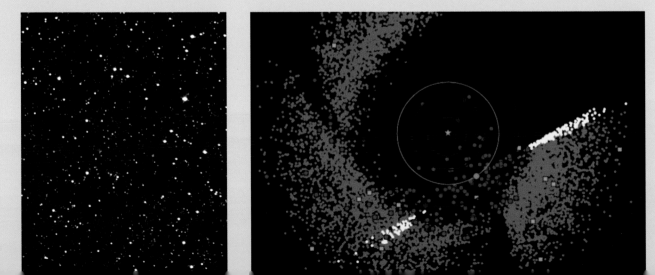

On the day NEOWISE was reactivated, the infrared telescope detected main belt asteroid (872) Holda as it moved across the sky. This composite shows its movement over time as red dots along its travel path.

This graphic shows the seventy-two near-Earth objects NEOWISE discovered (green dots) and the 439 other asteroids it characterized (gray dots) in the two years after the mission was restarted in 2013.

to learn more about near-Earth objects that could threaten our planet.

For the first six days, the telescope detected nothing new. Then, NEOWISE picked out a moving object that had never been seen before. As the spacecraft circled Earth, the scientists scanned the object several more times. It was an asteroid, extremely dark, like a lump of coal. But the lump was almost a half mile (800 m) across. They tracked the orbit and found that though it was about twenty-seven million miles (43 million km) from Earth, its orbit would bring it as close as three hundred thousand miles (482,803 km) from our planet. Named 2013 YP139, the object was a potentially hazardous near-Earth asteroid that would probably never have been spotted from telescopes on the ground. "It was a pretty great New Year's gift," Amy says.

NEOWISE continues to whip around the Earth, making it all the way around our planet every hour and a half. Every few days, after their computer collects and processes the photos, the NEOWISE team reviews them for asteroids. "We're not a big NASA mission," Amy says. "We're pretty small as these things go. But small is beautiful. We don't need fancy facilities to make important discoveries."

As with Catalina's ground-based telescopes, NEOWISE's results have a black background. The team is looking for white dots moving across the darkness. "The computer can do a lot of the work," says Amy. "We save the people for where we really need them the most, to make distinctions between the things

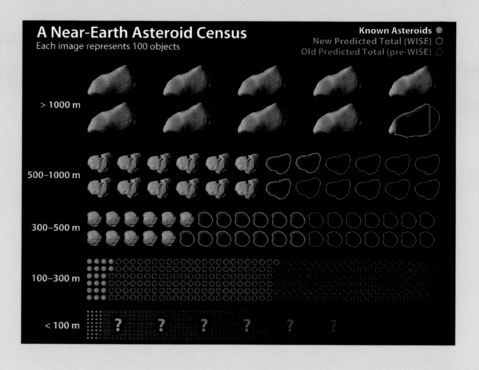

the computer has a hard time telling apart. It's really hard to beat a human at telling whether a dot is a real asteroid or not."

"Well, here's one!" says team member Joe Masiero. He spins his laptop around so everyone can see it.

When anyone on the team sees something that might be an asteroid, they send a flurry of emails to each other. "Look at this!" they write. Or "What do you think of this one?" Or "Check out this cool one."

"It's like panning for gold," says Carrie Nugent, another team member. "It could be gold, or it could be fool's gold."

"We don't want to be the team that cries wolf about something that turns out not to be an asteroid," Amy explains. "We have to be reliable."

Everyone agrees that Joe's find looks real. He runs it

NEOWISE team members Joe Masiero and Carrie Nugent study new images from the NEOWISE telescope.

through asteroids listed at the Minor Planet Center. "It doesn't correspond with anything known," he says. It's a new discovery.

"We're also doing a lot of characterizing asteroids," Amy says. "Whether they are known or unknown, we love them all. Our job is to measure their size and how reflective their surfaces are—how light or dark—which tells us a little about what they're made of." Lighter asteroids are usually rocky. Darker ones are a mix of darker carbon-bearing minerals and rock that tend to be more fragile and crumbly.

"A very, very important part is trying to understand the composition," Amy says. "For science—and for planetary defense."

But the mission's days are numbered. The spacecraft's orbit naturally shifts over time. "Eventually, we won't be able to keep the sunlight out of the telescope," Amy says. When NEOWISE's telescope gets too hot, it won't be able to sense warm objects even nearby.

However, Amy and her team know this is not the time to quit—there are so many more asteroids left to find. They are hoping to build a brand-new telescope. Like the NEOWISE spacecraft, it would use an infrared telescope. But it would cover fifteen times more of the sky with each photo. And instead of relying on frozen hydrogen to keep the telescope at the correct temperature, they have designed a tall shield to protect the instrument from the sun's rays.

After the new spacecraft—called NEOCam—is placed into orbit near Earth, it would keep an eye on the comings and goings of near-Earth asteroids all day and all night. "This placement is a great vantage point to watch near the sun," says Amy, "where most of the hazardous asteroids spend a lot of time."

This amazing new infrared asteroid-hunting telescope is

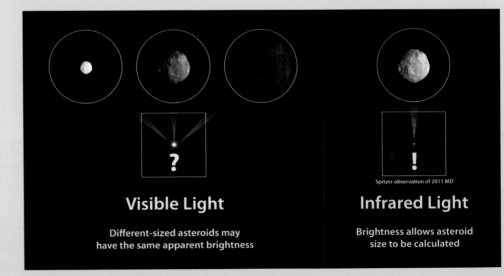

Visible Light
Different-sized asteroids may have the same apparent brightness

Infrared Light
Spitzer observation of 2011 MD
Brightness allows asteroid size to be calculated

expected to find *ten times* more near-Earth objects than have been discovered so far. Just five years after launch, it could pinpoint the location, orbits, and size of least *two-thirds* of the city-destroying-size asteroids—and the compositions of the most dangerous ones.

But what will be done if NEOCam finds a city-buster careening toward us?

That is something scientists are still trying to figure out.

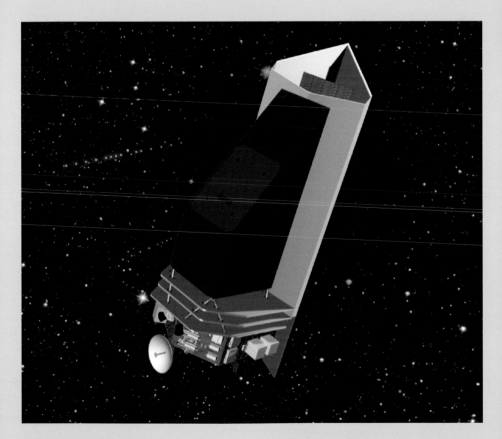

An artist's concept of the NEOCam infrared telescope, which is designed to search for asteroids near Earth's orbit.

SPACE SEARCHER AMY MAINZER

When Amy Mainzer was just seven years old, she devoured Greek mythology books. Looking through an encyclopedia one day, she realized that some Greek characters and some objects in space shared the same names. "When I understood the double meaning of words like 'Andromeda'—that it was both a princess from Greek mythology and a galaxy—I really wanted to learn more," she says.

Amy was always curious about how things are connected, how things work, how humans fit in. She explored plants and birds and rocks in her family's garden and then read books and stories about how they came to be. She got hooked on astronomy by reading about the Voyager spacecraft as it soared by Jupiter, Saturn, Uranus, and Neptune.

"I love that science is all about asking basic questions," she says. "You don't need to be Einstein to ask, 'How many asteroids are there in our solar system?' and 'Where are they?'"

NEOWISE principal investigator Amy Mainzer awaits images from their space telescope in the conference room near mission control.

Chapter Seven

HOW TO SAVE THE WORLD

On June 19, 2004, an asteroid survey in Hawaii discovered a quarter-mile-wide (400 m) near-Earth asteroid whose orbit crossed Earth's path twice every 323 days.

Projecting orbits into the future, astronomers noticed something frightening. On April 13, 2029, the asteroid, which was bigger than the one that formed the massive Meteor Crater, would fly quite close to Earth, possibly even near enough to smash into it.

Astronomers monitored the asteroid as it swung by Earth that December. On the twenty-fourth, as they tracked it and ran computer calculations, they estimated that the chance of the asteroid hitting our planet in 2029 was 1 in 300. As more

An artist's rendering of the asteroid Apophis, which generated worldwide concern because of its predicted close approaches to Earth.

data came in, they upped the odds to 1 in 63. By December 25, they predicted a 1 in 45 chance of a collision.

Named Apophis, after the Egyptian god "the uncreator," the asteroid was the first to get a rating of 4 on the Torino Scale, suggesting it was an asteroid "meriting concern." NASA reported that Apophis was "being tracked very carefully by many astronomers around the world."

HOW DANGEROUS IS AN ASTEROID?

THE TORINO SCALE
Assessing Asteroid Impact Predictions

Category	Level	Description
No Hazard	0	The likelihood of collision is zero, or is so low as to be effectively zero. Also applies to small objects such as meteors and bolides that burn up in the atmosphere as well as infrequent meteorite falls that rarely cause damage.
Normal	1	A routine discovery in which a pass near the Earth is predicted that poses no unusual level of danger. Current calculations show the chance of collision is extremely unlikely with no cause for public attention or public concern. New telescopic observations very likely will lead to re-assignment to Level 0.
Meriting Attention by Astronomers	2	A discovery, which may become routine with expanded searches, of an object making a somewhat close but not highly unusual pass near the Earth. While meriting attention by astronomers, there is no cause for public attention or public concern as an actual collision is very unlikely. New telescopic observations very likely will lead to re-assignment to Level 0.
	3	A close encounter, meriting attention by astronomers. Current calculations give a 1% or greater chance of collision capable of localized destruction. Most likely, new telescopic observations will lead to re-assignment to Level 0. Attention by the public and by public officials is merited if the encounter is less than a decade away.
	4	A close encounter, meriting attention by astronomers. Current calculations give a 1% or greater chance of collision capable of regional devastation. Most likely, new telescopic observations will lead to re-assignment to Level 0. Attention by the public and by public officials is merited if the encounter is less than a decade away.
Threatening	5	A close encounter posing a serious, but still uncertain threat of regional devastation. Critical attention by astronomers is needed to determine conclusively whether or not a collision will occur. If the encounter is less than a decade away, governmental contingency planning may be warranted.
	6	A close encounter by a large object posing a serious, but still uncertain threat of a global catastrophe. Critical attention by astronomers is needed to determine conclusively whether or not a collision will occur. If the encounter is less than three decades away, governmental contingency planning may be warranted.
	7	A very close encounter by a large object, which if occurring this century, poses an unprecedented but still uncertain threat of a global catastrophe. For such a threat in this century, international contingency planning is warranted, especially to determine urgently and conclusively whether or not a collision will occur.
Certain Collisions	8	A collision is certain, capable of causing localized destruction for an impact over land or possibly a tsunami if close offshore. Such events occur on average between once per 50 years and once per several 1,000 years.
	9	A collision is certain, capable of causing unprecedented regional devastation for a land impact or the threat of a major tsunami for an ocean impact. Such events occur on average between once per 10,000 years and once per 100,000 years.
	10	A collision is certain, capable of causing a global climatic catastrophe that may threaten the future of civilization as we know it, whether impacting land or ocean. Such events occur on average once per 100,000 years, or less often.

When scientists first calculated Apophis's orbit, they could forecast only a broad area where it might go. The longer and more frequently scientists observed it, the better they could narrow down its likely path. As professional and amateur astronomers around the globe carefully followed the asteroid, experts recommended that people remain calm: "In all likelihood, the possibility of impact will eventually be eliminated as the asteroid continues to be tracked . . ."

And they were correct. Vishnu Reddy, a research scientist at the Planetary Science Institute, and other astronomers confirmed that although Apophis would be barely visible to the naked eye on April 13, 2029—as a faint point of light moving quickly across the sky—the space boulder would not crash into Earth.

When Vishnu Reddy was growing up in India, his town had electricity for only a few hours each day. "In the nighttime we had absolutely nothing to do," he recalls. So he and his sisters climbed to the roof of their house and watched the stars. "The sky was so dark, you could see things without a telescope or binoculars. It was just beautiful."

In high school, he saved up money and spent a summer building a small telescope. Though he pursued other careers, working in Bollywood (India's movie industry) and as a journalist, Vishnu continued to build telescopes and study the solar system as an amateur astronomer.

Then one day he heard a presentation about how dangerous even small asteroids can be. "The astronomer said that it's very important that Indians study and discover asteroids because the country is surrounded by water on three sides," Vishnu recalls. "If there were a giant asteroid impact, the tsunami it caused would kill a lot of people."

Vishnu asked: "Can amateur astronomers do anything about it?"

The scientist answered: "Yeah, if you have a decent telescope, you can discover asteroids."

Vishnu scraped together the money for a better telescope, scheduled time on public telescopes, and as an amateur, discovered twenty-three new asteroids and helped figure out the orbits for thousands of others. Eventually, Vishnu got a Ph.D. Vishnu and his wife, Lucille Le Corre, who are now both research scientists at the Planetary Science Institute in Tucson, spend much of their time trying to match meteorites to their parent bodies—in other words, figuring out where meteorites came from in the solar system. Did they come from the moon? Mars? A large asteroid like Ceres or Vesta or a cluster of asteroids that were once one huge space rock?

It's a scientific game of "Are You My Mother?"

"We must make the connection between what we find on Earth and what we find in the sky," says Vishnu. "If something is going to hit Earth, what is it made of? The composition and size of an object has direct implications for how much damage there might be on the ground."

Vishnu Reddy (left) and Lucille Le Corre own a huge fourteen-inch (36 cm) telescope that sits on a second-floor balcony off their bedroom in Tucson, Arizona. Lucille's expertise is in space-based astronomy—learning about the solar system from spacecraft in space. Vishnu's experience is ground-based. "Now we use both," Lucille says. "We use astronomy as a tool to do geology and geology as a tool to do astronomy."

What if the asteroid trackers *had* confirmed that Apophis, or another asteroid, was on a collision course with our planet? How could we avoid the horrifying destruction that happened at Meteor Crater or, even worse, Chicxulub?

BOMB IT!

The most obvious solution, the one people think of first: blow up the asteroid. "We could probably build a hydrogen bomb big enough to blow one up," says David Kring. "But bombing is just as likely to fragment an asteroid, not stop it from striking. And a spray of shotgun fragments can be more destructive than a single bullet."

Another idea is to detonate a bomb off to one side of an asteroid. The part facing the bomb would heat and vaporize, sending the asteroid in the other direction. Or if the explosion were even farther away, shock waves could move the asteroid. But again, the explosion could break up the asteroid into large pieces, making the problem worse instead of solving it.

"It all depends on the composition of the asteroid," says Vishnu Reddy. To really understand how any method would work on a particular asteroid, we have to know more about its makeup, he says. Scientists must consider whether an intervention will break up or disperse asteroid chunks in unexpected and dangerous ways.

This artist's concept of a bombed asteroid shows how a space rock may shatter, causing multiple impacts.

CRASH INTO IT!

Some experts, like Amy Mainzer, think crashing a spacecraft into a dangerous asteroid might be a more promising approach. "We've done something similar before,"

she says. In July 2005, NASA's Deep Impact spacecraft sent a contraption the size of an average coffee table careening into an 820-pound (370 kg) comet. Though they don't know if the impact affected the comet's orbit, they did hit where they wanted to—and left a five-hundred-foot-wide (150 m) crater on the comet to show for it.

NASA and the European Space Agency are joining forces to further test the idea of crashing an asteroid off course. In October 2020, they will launch two spacecraft to the binary asteroids Didymoon and Didymos. These asteroids orbit each other close to Earth. The European scientists will send a lander to the smaller of the two, the 525-foot-wide (160 m) Didymoon, to study what it's made of and how dense it is. Then the lander will steer NASA's Double Asteroid Redirection Test spacecraft to smash right into Didymoon. Scientists hope the impact will bump both asteroids off their orbits.

NASA's Deep Impact probe collides with the comet Tempel 1. This photo was taken by the spacecraft that sent the probe hurtling toward the comet.

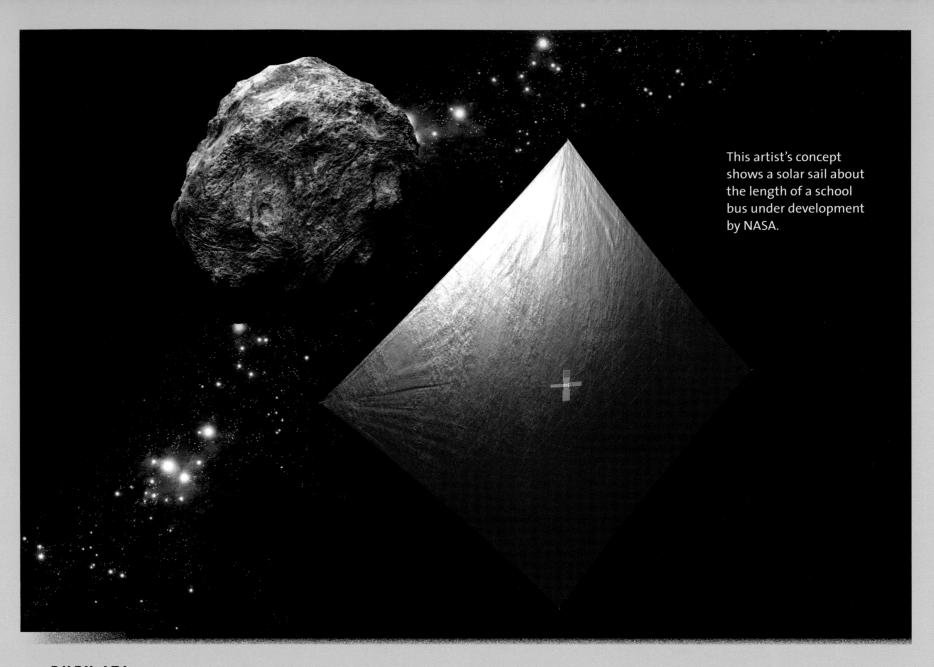

This artist's concept shows a solar sail about the length of a school bus under development by NASA.

PUSH IT! A variation on the "crash into it" approach is to find a gentler way to nudge the asteroid off course. One idea would require building a contraption on the asteroid that would hurl rocks into space. That throwing motion could propel the asteroid in the other direction, like the recoil from a rifle. Likewise, we could attach rockets to an asteroid, so when they blasted off, they would thrust the asteroid away.

Scientists also envision solar rays pushing huge solar sails, which would then push an asteroid. The solar-sails idea is based on the fact that solar heat creates radiation pressure. Light in

This artist's rendering demonstrates Sung Wook Paek's idea of how one barrage of paint spatters would cover half an asteroid, and then, as the asteroid rotated, a second barrage would coat the other half.

color, super lightweight, and a hundred times thinner than a piece of paper, these sails could be hitched to a dangerous asteroid. The constant pressure of photons pushing on the sail could shove the asteroid off course.

Another proposal suggests coating an asteroid in bright white paint or wrapping it in highly reflective aluminum foil, like a huge baked potato. More photons from the radiation would bounce off the asteroid, pushing it ever so slowly away from the sun. Even a small change in pressure would gradually nudge the threatening asteroid off its orbit.

SHOOT IT! Sung Wook Paek, a graduate student at the Massachusetts Institute of Technology, proposes firing rounds of paint-ball pellets full of white powder at the target asteroid. The barrage of pellets would start to drive the asteroid off its course. Photons from the sun bouncing off the white paint would do the rest. Sung estimates his spacecraft would have to shoot five tons of paint-ball pellets to slowly nudge an asteroid the size and composition of Apophis off its trajectory.

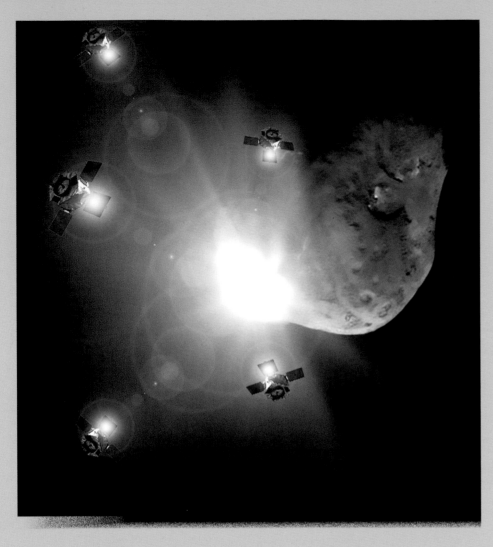

An artist's rendition of the laser concept shows multiple spacecraft swarming around a dangerous asteroid, shooting it off course. This illustration uses an actual image of comet Tempel 1 to represent the threatening object and an artist's concept of NASA's Van Allen Probe spacecraft to represent the lasers.

VAPORIZE IT! Another way of pushing is to scorch one side of the asteroid. The vaporized material would propel the asteroid away from the heat source. Ideas include reflecting sunlight from a huge space mirror or a swarm of small mirror-bearing spacecraft onto the threatening asteroid or by zapping it with a powerful space laser. Some scientists propose sending a fleet of small spacecraft equipped with lasers to nudge the asteroid right where scientists want it to go.

TUG IT! People have even floated the idea of making a huge lasso or a giant bag so a spacecraft could grab an entire asteroid and haul it into orbit around the moon. Others have suggested attaching a giant tether to an asteroid with a huge weight on the other end to act like an anchor, slowing the asteroid down. "There is no shortage of ideas about how to stop an asteroid," says Amy Mainzer.

Engineers are currently exploring ways to drag an asteroid off course without touching it. Called the "gravity tug," this option requires sending a massive spacecraft near enough to an asteroid that the gravity of the spacecraft's mass would move the asteroid forward, backward, or off its trajectory.

The gravity could pull an asteroid faster along its orbit so it crosses Earth's orbit before Earth is in the way. Or the gravity could pull the asteroid in the opposite direction, slowing its orbit down just enough to give Earth time to scoot by before the asteroid arrives. Amazingly, to avoid disaster, we only need to adjust an asteroid's arrival time by a mere three or four minutes.

A fifteen-person company called Tethers Unlimited won a $200,000 contract from NASA to develop a tiny twether—as thin as dental floss—to wrangle an asteroid off course.

This graphic depicts the Asteroid Redirect Mission's vehicle conducting a .6 mile (1 km) fly-by of its target asteroid.

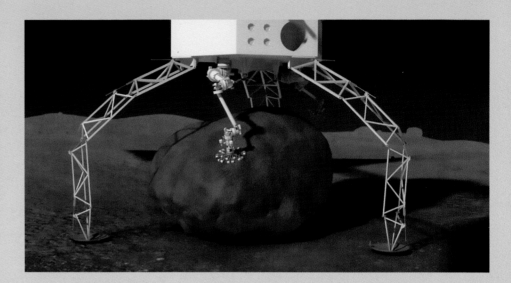

This artist's concept shows the Asteroid Capture Microspine grippers on the end of the robotics arms grasp and secure a boulder from the surface of the asteroid.

While the asteroid gravity tug hasn't been tried yet, it will get a dramatic test in the Asteroid Redirect Mission. ARM will launch a robotic spacecraft to a large near-Earth asteroid in December of 2020. After the spacecraft circles the asteroid, studying its surface for about a year, it will slowly descend onto the surface. Then it will wrap its three robotic arms around a thirteen-foot (4 m) boulder, much like the claw crane at an arcade reaching for a stuffed animal. The spacecraft will then push off, carrying the rock back into space.

Here is where the spacecraft with the boulder becomes a gravity tug. By flying along with the asteroid, staying on one side of it for 215 to 400 days, the combined gravity of the spacecraft and the boulder should tug the asteroid slightly off its orbit. Even a little shift could mean life or death for our planet if that asteroid were headed our way.

Though scientists and engineers no doubt have the talent and technology to prevent an asteroid from colliding with Earth, they will need time—lots of time. They need time to pinpoint the asteroid's size, shape, and composition. They need time to determine the dangerous asteroid's exact orbit. "It's hard to plan a campaign to move something if we don't know exactly where it is," Amy says.

They need time to develop and test ideas, time to build

Once the boulder is secured with a drill, the vehicle will hop off from the surface of the asteroid. Thrusters will push the craft back to space.

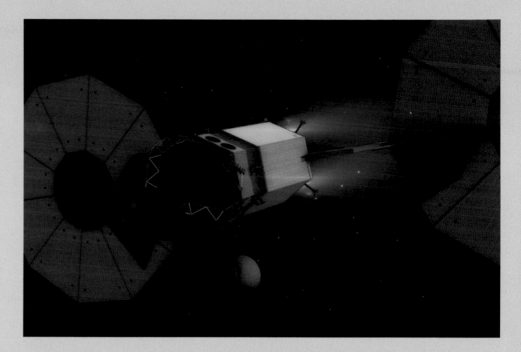

Before traveling toward a stable orbit around the moon, the ARM vehicle will fly near the main asteroid. Scientists hope that the weight of the spacecraft and the boulder will tug the main asteroid off its course.

the huge spacecraft and other equipment, and time to get to the threatening asteroid. And the safest, most reliable methods may require applying small amounts of force to the asteroid for a long, long time.

"The key to success: find them early, find them early, find them early," Amy says.

The good news is that 95 percent of the really big asteroids have already been discovered and tracked. "That's pretty fabulous and an amazing achievement," says Amy. "So now we don't have to worry about what happened to the dinosaurs. It's pretty unlikely to happen to us."

While there are still many smaller asteroids left to discover,

we have the power to find them. "The asteroid problem is something we can actually work on and make progress on," Amy says. "We can do something about it. We can go find the asteroids."

"If we put our minds and our money to it, we can do it," she says. "We really can."

WHAT YOU CAN DO!

Design and Test Asteroid Search and Destroy (or Deflect) Ideas

NASA'S Asteroid Grand Challenge has a mission to find *all* asteroid threats and figure out what to do about them. And they want *you* to get involved. They need amateur astronomers to find and track asteroids and people to come up with and test ideas to keep them from colliding with Earth. Start by exploring the project's webpage: www.nasa.gov/content/asteroid-grand-challenge. And sign up for the mailing list to keep up with opportunities. Maybe *you* will be part of saving our planet!

Discover an Asteroid

Catalina Sky Survey has set up a website where you can help hunt for asteroids. Called the Asteroid Zoo (asteroidzoo.org), the website lets you review sets of photos taken by the telescopes. Do you see distinct white dots moving from photo to photo? You may have discovered an asteroid!

Track an Asteroid

Join the OSIRIS-REx mission's Target Asteroids! citizen science program and track known near-Earth asteroids to help scientists learn more about them: www.asteroidmission.org/get-involved/target -asteroids.

You don't need a college degree to track asteroids with a telescope. It's not easy, but everything you need is explained on the Minor Planet Center's website page "Guide to Minor Body Astrometry": www.minorplanetcenter.net/iau/info/Astrometry.html.

For a list of recently discovered asteroids that need confirmation, visit www.minorplanetcenter.net/iau/NEO/toconfirm_tabular.html.

Spot a Fireball

If you see a moving flash in the sky, like a huge shooting star, it might be a fireball from a falling asteroid. Your observation could help scientists track and study the fall—and maybe even recover a meteorite. Watch carefully and note these details:

- The time.
- The time between the meteor's appearance and disappearance.
- Any colors, whether pieces broke off, and whether the meteor had a glowing trail.
- Any sounds you hear.
- The meteor's location. Use references such as power lines, poles, chimneys, trees, or hills to identify where you first saw the meteor and where you last saw it. Note your exact location using a map or GPS. Estimate the compass direction where the fireball fell. If you know star names or constellations, use them for reference as well.

Report the sighting to the American Meteor Society at www .amsmeteors.org/members/imo/report_intro.

Tips for Meteorite Collecting

- By law in the United States, meteorites belong to the owner of the land they fall on. You can hunt them—and keep them—only with the owner's permission.
- Most meteorites from recent falls have a dull, dark black fusion crust. Some may have a glassy black crust. Over time, the crust may rust to reddish brown.
- Some meteorites will look pockmarked with smooth, thumb-print-like depressions that formed as the asteroid passed through the atmosphere.
- Most meteorites have some metal in them and will be attracted to a magnet. (Some hunters use metal detectors.)

- Most meteorites are dense, more than three times heavier than Earth rocks of the same size.
- Take a picture of the meteorite before you pick it up, and note its exact location.
- Use gloves or a plastic bag to pick up the meteorite so you don't transfer oils or moisture from your hands.
- Don't put meteorites in your pocket—they could be delicate and break.
- If you suspect you have found a meteorite, check out these sites to learn how to confirm the discovery: meteorites.wustl.edu; meteorite.unm.edu/meteorites/meteorite-museum/how-id -meteorite; and geology.com/meteorites/meteorite-identification .shtml.

LEARN MORE ABOUT ASTEROIDS AND METEORITES

Read More

Bortz, Alfred B. *Collision Course!: Cosmic Impacts and Life on Earth.* Brookfield, Conn.: Millbrook Press, 2001.

Carson, Mary Kay. *Far-Out Guide to Asteroids and Comets.* Berkeley Heights, N.J.: Bailey Books, 2011.

Henderson, Douglas. *Asteroid Impact.* New York: Dial, 2000.

Kelley, J. A. *Meteor Showers.* New York: Scholastic, 2010.

Miller, Ron. *Asteroids, Comets, and Meteors.* Minneapolis, MN: Twenty-First Century Books, 2006.

Riggs, Kate. *Across the Universe: Asteroids.* Mankato, MN: Creative Education, 2015.

Search More

Fireballs and Meteors

Read witness accounts of recently spotted fireballs on the American Meteor Society's fireball report page.

www.amsmeteors.org/category/fireball-sightings

View a map of the latest twenty-five meteors spotted worldwide.

lunarmeteoritehunters.blogspot.com

Find out when the next meteor showers are going to happen.

earthsky.org/astronomy-essentials/earthskys-meteor-shower-guide

Meteorite Collections

Center for Meteorite Studies at Arizona State University

meteorites.asu.edu

Falling Rocks Meteorite Collection

www.fallingrocks.com/collection.htm

Field Museum, Chicago, Illinois

www.fieldmuseum.org

International Meteorite Collectors Association

imca.cc

Museum of Natural History, London

www.nhm.ac.uk/our-science/collections/mineralogy-collections /meteorites-collection.html

Natural History Museum, Los Angeles

www.nhm.org/site/research-collections/mineral-sciences/view -collections

Robert Ward Collection

robertwardmeteorites.com

Smithsonian National Museum of Natural History, Meteorite Gallery

geogallery.si.edu/index.php/meteorites

Meteorite Hunting

Explore Doppler radar images at the National Oceanic and Atmospheric Administration's National Weather Service.

www.weather.gov/radar

Read about meteorite hunter Robert Ward's adventures meteorite hunting and view samples of his collection.

robertwardmeteorites.com

Learn how to figure out if you have found a real meteorite.

meteorites.wustl.edu

meteorite.unm.edu/meteorites/meteorite-museum/how-id-meteorite

geology.com/meteorites/meteorite-identification.shtml

Asteroid Surveys

Catalina Sky Survey

www.lpl.arizona.edu/css

Panoramic Survey Telescope and Rapid Response System (PAN-STARRS)

pan-starrs.ifa.hawaii.edu/public

Spacewatch

spacewatch.lpl.arizona.edu

Asteroids Discovered

Learn about the next five known asteroids that will be making close approaches to Earth.

www.nasa.gov/mission_pages/asteroids/widget/index.html

Follow the tally of asteroids discovered to date and a list of close approaches.

minorplanetcenter.net/about

Check out NASA's list of asteroids that have a risk of impact with Earth.

neo.jpl.nasa.gov/risks

Also view the Minor Planet Center's list of potentially hazardous asteroids.

www.minorplanetcenter.org/iau/lists/Dangerous.html

Asteroid Space Missions

Asteroid Impact and Deflection Assessment (AIDA) mission

www.nasa.gov/planetarydefense/aida

Asteroid Redirect Mission

www.nasa.gov/content/what-is-nasa-s-asteroid-redirect-mission

Dawn mission to Vesta and Ceres

dawn.jpl.nasa.gov

Deep Impact Mission

www.nasa.gov/mission_pages/deepimpact/main/#.VyENv0eHh9Y

Hayabusa 2 sample return mission to asteroid Ryugu

global.jaxa.jp/projects/sat/hayabusa2

NEOCam

neocam.ipac.caltech.edu

NEOWISE

neo.jpl.nasa.gov/programs/neowise.html

www.jpl.nasa.gov/multimedia/wise

OSIRIS-REx sample return mission to the asteroid Bennu

www.asteroidmission.org

Impact Craters

About impact craters

www.lpi.usra.edu/education/explore/shaping_the_planets/impact_cratering.shtml

Chicxulub

www.lpi.usra.edu/science/kring/epo_web/impact_cratering/Chicxulub

Meteor Crater

meteorcrater.com

Planetary Defense: Asteroid Deflection and Destruction

B612 is a private organization focused on protecting Earth from asteroid impacts.

b612foundation.org

"Every Way Devised to Deflect an Asteroid"

www.universetoday.com/90798/every-way-devised-to-deflect-an-asteroid

Laser Bees

www.planetary.org/explore/projects/laser-bees

"Paintballs May Deflect an Incoming Asteroid"

news.mit.edu/2012/deflecting-an-asteroid-with-paintballs-1026

"Ten Ways to Stop a Killer Asteroid"

science.howstuffworks.com/10-ways-to-stop-asteroid.htm

"Top 10 Ways to Stop an Asteroid"

www.seeker.com/top-10-ways-to-stop-an-asteroid-1766426958.html#news.discovery.com

Other Asteroid Sites of Interest

Asteroid Apophis

neo.jpl.nasa.gov/apophis

Asteroid belt

space-facts.com/asteroid-belt

Asteroid news

www.sciencedaily.com/videos/space_time/asteroids,_comets_and_meteors

Asteroid video collection

www.nasa.gov/mission_pages/asteroids/videos/index.html

Astronomy for Teens

astronoteen.org

Killer Asteroids (simulate an asteroid impact in your town, nudge an asteroid off its course, and other activities)

www.killerasteroids.org

GLOSSARY

achondrite: a type of stony meteorite without chondrules, or round mineral grains.

asteroid: a space rock orbiting the sun.

asteroid belt: an area where many space rocks orbit the sun. The main asteroid belt in our solar system lies between Mars and Jupiter.

astronomer: a scientist who studies space.

atmosphere: a layer of gases surrounding a planet held in place by gravity.

chondrite: a type of stony meteorite with round mineral grains called chondrules.

collision course: a path that will cause an object to hit another object.

ecliptic: the plane on which the Earth orbits the sun.

ejecta: material that is thrown when an asteroid strikes a planet and makes a crater.

fireball: a very bright meteor caused when an asteroid falls through the atmosphere.

fusion crust: the blackened outer layer of a meteorite created when the surface of an asteroid falling through the atmosphere melts and then cools.

geocentric: orbiting the Earth.

heliocentric: orbiting the sun.

impact crater: a roughly circular depression on the surface of a planet created when an object such as an asteroid hits at high speed.

infrared: heat rays; radiant energy past the red end of the visible spectrum.

iron meteorites: space rocks full of iron-nickel metal.

lunar distance: the distance between Earth and the moon—239,000 miles (385,000 km) on average.

meteor: the streak of light visible when a space rock glows from the friction of moving through Earth's atmosphere; commonly known as a shooting star.

meteor shower: an astronomical event that happens over a period of time when many small space rocks hit the Earth's atmosphere at high speeds, causing flashes of light to move across the sky.

meteorite: a piece of an asteroid that survives a trip through the Earth's atmosphere and lands on the ground.

micrometeorite: a tiny piece of material from space, smaller than .08 inch (2 mm), that survives a trip through the Earth's atmosphere.

near-Earth asteroid: an asteroid whose orbit brings it close to Earth's neighborhood, within the area roughly 120,800,000 miles (194,500,000 km) from the sun.

near-Earth object: an asteroid or comet whose orbit brings it close to Earth's neighborhood within the area roughly 120,800,000 miles (194,500,000 km) from the sun.

NEOWISE: a NASA space mission that searched for near-Earth asteroids using data from the infrared telescope on the Wide-field Infrared Survey Explorer (WISE) spacecraft.

NEOCam: a new NASA space project with a mission to find and characterize two-thirds of the near-Earth objects larger than 459 feet (140 m) using an infrared telescope and a wide-field camera operating at thermal infrared wavelengths on a spacecraft orbiting Earth.

orbit: the path of an object around a point in space; the curved path a planet takes around the sun.

photons: tiny particles of light.

plume: smoke, steam, or a collection of dust that trails behind a meteor or fireball, also known as a "train."

potentially hazardous asteroid (PHA): any asteroid more than 350 feet (110 m) wide whose orbit brings it within roughly 4,700,000 miles (7,500,000 km) of Earth's orbit, thus having the potential to hit Earth and cause damage.

radiation pressure: the force exerted by energy from the sun.

satellite: an object orbiting a planet; moons are considered satellites, as are spacecraft that are placed into orbit.

shock wave: a rapid compression in the air or other medium caused by an explosion or an object traveling faster than the speed of sound.

spectra: the pattern of radiation given off by rocks, which is determined by their compositions.

spectrometer: an instrument that measures the radiation given by a rock to determine what elements or minerals make up the rock.

stony meteorites: space rocks made mostly from silicate (a silicon compound) minerals, as are most rocks on Earth.

stony-iron meteorites: space rocks made from a roughly equal mix of silicates and iron-nickel metals.

trajectory: the path a moving object is expected to follow.

MANY THANKS

To all the asteroid and meteorite hunters and scientists who shared their expertise and experiences with me, thank you for your out-of-this-world contributions: Eric Christensen, the principal investigator for Catalina Sky Survey; Marc Fries, a research scientist with NASA's Johnson Space Center; Dolores Hill, scientist at the Lunar and Planetary Laboratory at the University of Arizona; David Kring, senior scientist at the Lunar and Planetary Institute; Lucille Le Corre, research scientist at the Planetary Science Institute; Amy Mainzer, principal investigator for NEOWISE and NEOCam, and team members Beth Fabinsky, Joe Masiero, and Carrie Nugent; Vishnu Reddy, research scientist at the Planetary Science Institute; Robert and Anne Marie Ward, meteorite hunters; and Linda Welzenbach, former meteorite curator for the Smithsonian.

Thank you to my friend and photographer Karin Anderson for meeting me wherever we needed to go to bring this story to life visually; to friend and editor Cynthia Platt for helping me organize and trim the massive amount of fascinating information available on this topic; and to friend and intern Elizabeth Goss for help with background and photo research. You have all had a massive impact on this book.

Finally, thank you to all my brilliant reader-writer friends for their stellar insights: Addie Boswell, Melissa Dalton, Ruth Tenzer Feldman, Ellen Howard, Barbara Kerley, Amber Keyser, Amy Loy, Sara Ryan, Nicole Marie Schreiber, and Emily Whitman.

I thank my lucky stars to have worked with you all!

NOTES

All of the quotations and descriptions come from interviews and site visits with the named scientists except the following:

2   "We got an awful . . .": BBC News, "Russia Meteor Eyewitness."

"Windows were blown . . .": *Russia Today*, "'Shock and Frustration.'"

"Many of us were thinking . . .": Broad, "Crater Supports Extinction Theory."

3   "It is a nightmare . . .": *Russia Today*, "'Shock and Frustration.'"

"I saw this terrible . . .": *Russia Today*, "'Shock and Frustration.'"

"Now green men . . .": Englund, "After the Meteor."

9   "It was like a huge firework . . .": American Meteor Society, Event 2635-2015, Report 2635ee from Val W.

15   The analysis of the Creston meteorite was conducted by Laurence Garvie, Center for Meteorite Studies, Arizona State University.

43   "That's enough time . . .": Institute for Astronomy, University of Hawaii, "ATLAS: The Asteroid Terrestrial-impact Last Alert System."

53   "Being tracked . . .": Britt, "Asteroid with Chance of Hitting Earth in 2029 Now Being Watched 'Very Carefully.'"

54   "In all likelihood . . .": Britt, "Asteroid with Chance of Hitting Earth in 2029 Now Being Watched 'Very Carefully.'"

58–59 Information on solar sails: Bonsor, "How Solar Sails Work."

59   Information on coating or wrapping an asteroid: Wall, "Deflecting Killer Asteroids Away from Earth."

Information on the paint-ball method: Space.com staff, "How Paintballs Could Save Earth from Giant Asteroids."

60–62 Information on the gravity tug: Schweickart et al., "The Asteroid Tugboat."

SOURCES

American Meteor Society. Fireball Logs. Event 2635-2015. www.amsmeteors.org/members/imo_view/event/2015/2635

BBC News. "Russia Meteor Eyewitness: 'Something Like the Sun Fell.'" BBC.com, February 15, 2013. www.bbc.com/news/world-europe -21471942.

Bonsor, Kevin. "How Solar Sails Work." HowStuffWorks.com, October 12, 2000. science.howstuffworks.com/solar-sail.htm.

Britt, Robert Roy. "Asteroid with Chance of Hitting Earth in 2029 Now Being Watched 'Very Carefully.'" Space.com, December 24, 2004. www.space.com/622-asteroid-chance-hitting-earth-2029-watched -carefully.html.

Broad, William J. "Crater Supports Extinction Theory." *New York Times*, August 14, 1992, A12.

Christensen, Eric. Principal investigator for Catalina Sky Survey. Observatory visit with author March 2015 and emails 2015–16.

Englund, Will. "After the Meteor, Some in Chelyabinsk Prepare to Clean Up." *Washington Post*, February 16, 2013.

———. "Visitor from Space Breaks Apart in the Air Over Chelyabinsk; Shock Wave Smashes Homes and Factories." *Washington Post*, February 15, 2013.

Fabinsky, Beth. NEOWISE and NEOCAM team member. Site visit with author to Jet Propulsion Laboratory, February 2016.

Fries, Marc. Research scientist with NASA's Johnson Space Center. Meteorite hunt in Creston, California, with author December 2015 and emails 2015–16.

Fries, Marc, and Jeffrey Fries. "Doppler Weather Radar as a Meteorite Recovery Tool." *Meteoritics and Planetary Science* 45, no. 9 (2010): 1476–87.

Hill, Dolores. Scientist at the Lunar and Planetary Laboratory at the University of Arizona. Laboratory visit with author March 2015 and emails 2015–16.

Institute for Astronomy, University of Hawaii. "ATLAS: The Asteroid Terrestrial-impact Last Alert System." Press release, February 15, 2013.

Kring, David. Senior scientist at the Lunar and Planetary Institute. Site visit with author in Meteor Crater March 2015 and emails 2015–16.

———. "Blast from the Past." *Astronomy*, August 2006, 46–51.

———. "The Chicxulub Impact Event and Its Environmental Consequences at the Cretaceous-Tertiary Boundary." *Palaeogeography, Palaeoclimatology, Palaeoecology* 255, no. 1 (2007): 4–21.

———. *Guidebook to the Geology of Barringer Meteorite Crater, Arizona (a.k.a. Meteor Crater)*. Houston, Texas: Lunar and Planetary Institute, 2007.

———. "Unlocking the Solar System's Past." *Astronomy*, August 2006, 32–37.

Kring, David, and Mark Boslough. "Chelyabinsk: Portrait of an Asteroid Airburst." *Physics Today* 6, no. 9 (2014): 32.

Kring, David, and Daniel A. Durda. "The Day the World Burned." *Scientific American*, December 2003, 98–105.

Le Corre, Lucille. Research scientist at the Planetary Science Institute. In-person interview with author, March 2015.

Mainzer, Amy. Principal investigator for NEOWISE and NEOCAM. Phone interview, in-person interview, emails, and site visit with author to Jet Propulsion Laboratory, 2015–16.

Masiero, Joseph. NEOWISE and NEOCAM team member. Site visit with author to Jet Propulsion Laboratory, February 2016.

NASA/JPL Near-Earth Object Program Office. "First Asteroid Discovered in 2014 Has Impact (2014 AA)." NASA. Press release, January 2, 2014. neo.jpl.nasa.gov/news/news182.html.

Nugent, Carrie. NEOWISE and NEOCAM team member. Site visit with author to Jet Propulsion Laboratory, February 2016.

Reddy, Vishnu. Research scientist at the Planetary Science Institute. In-person interview March 2015 and emails 2015–16.

Russia Today. "'Shock and Frustration': Locals Report on Meteorite Crash in Russian Urals." RT.com, February 15, 2013. rt.com/news/chelyabinsk-meteorite-witness-report-285.

Schweickart, Russell, Edward Lu, Piet Hut, and Clark Chapman. "The Asteroid Tugboat." *Scientific American*, November 2003. 57.

Space.com staff. "How Paintballs Could Save Earth from Giant Asteroids." *Space.com*. October 26, 2012. www.space.com/18248-paintballs-asteroid-impact-deflection-video.html

Tonry, John. Project lead for the Asteroid Terrestrial Last Alert System, Institute for Astronomy, University of Hawaii. Emails 2016.

Wall, Mike. "Deflecting Killer Asteroids Away from Earth: How We Could Do It." *Space.com* November 7, 2011. www.space.com/13524-deflecting-killer-asteroids-earth-impact-methods.html

Ward, Anne Marie. Meteorite hunter. In-person interviews March 2015; meteorite hunt in Creston, California, with author December 2015; emails 2015–16.

Ward, Robert. Meteorite hunter. In-person interviews March 2015; meteorite hunt in Creston, California, with author December 2015; emails 2015–16.

Welzenbach, Linda. Former meteorite curator for the Smithsonian and current research scientist for the Planetary Science Institute. Meteorite hunt in Creston, California, with author December 2015 and emails 2015–16.

PHOTO CREDITS

Mopic/Shutterstock: 52–53, front jacket

NASA: 58, 62, 63

NASA/Bill Ingalls: 1 (background)

NASA/JPL: 56–57 (middle)

NASA/JPL-Caltech: 6, 42, 47 (top and bottom right), 49, 50 (bottom left), 51 (left)

NASA/JPL-Caltech/UCLA: 46–47

NASA/JPL-Caltech UMD: 57 (right)

NASA/Christie Maddock/Elizabeth Goss: 60

NEOWISE/NASA/JPL: 48 (left)

Sung Wook Paek: 59

Nikita Plekhanov: 3 (middle)

Jeff Scovil: 13 (bottom left, middle, right)

The Asahi Shimbun via Getty Images: 3(right)

SRTM Team NASA/JPL/NIMA: 28

Tethers Unlimited, Inc.: 61

INDEX

Note: Page references in **bold** indicate text in photograph captions.

SCIENTISTS IN THE FIELD
WHERE SCIENCE MEETS ADVENTURE

Check out these titles to meet more scientists who are out in the field—and contributing every day to our knowledge of the world around us:

Looking for even more adventure? Craving updates on the work of your favorite scientists, as well as in-depth video footage, audio, photography, and more? Then visit the new Scientists in the Field website!

WWW.SCIENCEMEETSADVENTURE.COM